Contents

Introduction

What is the value of community for an old man who for a variety of reasons in the course of his life now finds himself without a best friend, a soul-mate, a significant other, a business partner, a bedmate, a co-dependent, a fellow addict, a woman in love, a comrade-in-arms: whatever you want to call the other blighter in the passenger seat of life's little journey? They have all flown the coop (or Coupe, to continue the car metaphor).

If there is nobody in particular for you, you have no choice but to go for people in general – the definition of society or community or, in even plainer language, you could say: people in groups.

There are three stages in life: young, middle and old. There are three levels of living: solitary, private and public, hence my trilogy culled from a daily diary devoted to this subject over a period of thirty years. So the three books are called *Self*, *Self & Self*, and *Self & Self & Self*.

My first book, *Self: The Spiritual Diet*, was all about the fact that ultimately you live by yourself. When you enter this life you are given a cloak of skin and there is no escaping it until you make your departure from this world at the moment of death and return to wherever you came from before you came here in the first place.

Physically, you are pinned down on this earth with several stone of flesh and blood, bones and organs. There is only one organ that does not weigh anything and that is the soul. Cynics say it is so light it does not even exist. The skin, which wraps you up like a present, not only keeps the ensemble together, it also serves to keep you apart from other people. And that is the nub of the matter. You are physically and mentally separate from the rest of the world and the job of life is to try and overcome that apparently unbridgeable gap.

My trilogy recommends three different strategies to cross that bridge. The first book was an attempt at trumping the essential solitude of man by conquering the law of gravity. You do this by sublimation. Can you raise your spirit so successfully that earthly distance is defeated? Or to put it crudely, can you bond with God? It is a bit like a metaphysical Higgs boson experiment.

So the book sees your intrepid explorer in the shape of a middle age man – who did not look unlike myself at that time following in the footsteps of great poets, thinkers, philosophers, mystics, theologians and anybody else who has got anything to say on the subject of spirituality – set himself the task of immersing himself in poetry, prayer and nature for 1000 days.

The book was a study in cause and effect. It sought to prove the existence or absence of the Lord in these three areas of creativity, through experience. I was putting God to the test. If I pray an hour a day for 1000 days, I expect results. If I go out and commune with nature for days at a stretch, I want to feel something other worldly. If I stick my head in a hundred poetry books, I want to get transported into a higher state of consciousness. Interesting experiment . . . Interesting book . . . It costs a tenner.

The second book which I call 'Self & Self' was published by Quartet Books as *The Joy of Talk* in 2010. The Bible's second commandment to man – the one immediately after the one that orders us to believe in God – and so the first practical piece of advice handed down from God to Man via Moses, is 'Love thy neighbour as thyself.' Well, to be honest, I personally do not have a problem with the second half of that commandment. I once confided in a friend of mine, Joe Gibbs, that rather an attractive woman had recently declared undying love for me. She had told me that she could not get me out of her mind and she thought about me all the time. I had sympathised with her and said: 'I quite understand.'

'You conceited buffoon!' exclaimed Joe, roaring with laughter. 'I'm surprised you didn't say: "Well, that make two of us!"'

My problem, which I think I share with the rest of humanity, is loving other people. I fancy lots of people. I quite like a few. But love is a big word and only now in old age, abandoned by everybody, do I really know what it means. Not that I am going to tell you now. It is a one word answer and I have dropped it like a pin in the haystack somewhere in the middle of this book. I deliver it when the time is right.

So my second book was all about trying to make real connection with your neighbour, which can blossom into love and realising the only way of doing it is by communication, primarily through words because that is the way us human beings do it. Inevitably, the book became a self-help book about the art of conversation.

Now we arrive at this book, the climax of the series. If I can call my two pubs a chain, I can call my three books a series. Remember the instruction about loving yourself. That can include inflationary declarations of self-worth, frankly . . . boasting.

The idea is that if you have succeeded in using the first book to develop a real spiritual life for yourself so that you are happy with yourself by yourself and you use the second book to learn how to concentrate on the most important thing in life in your dealings with other people, which is their conversation so that you see yourself happy in the company of other people on a one-to-one basis – you are now ready for the third book, whose aim is to make you happy in old age and the trick is learning how to live on the periphery, merely as part of a group.

It is a tall order and requires digging deep inside you a huge reservoir of humility into which you bury your ego and then flooding it with appreciation of other people. It is sort of the opposite effect of the first book. In *Self* you let fly your soul above the concerns of this world. In *Self & Self & Self,* you drown your ego in them.

Why is the subtitle of my third book; 'Old Age – My Three Best Friends: Alcohol, Television and God'? Where else do a group of people let their hair down to have a good time together but at a party? Who ever heard of a party without alcohol? Where else but on television does society tell you everything you would want to know about the way it feels and how it thinks? Where else does it so readily mix love and knowledge to make culture? Who else but God so loved the world that He sent down His Only Son to die for our sins?

How dare I write about God? If two fellows called Grimm could write fairy tales, I don't see why a miscreant like me can't write about God, and writing as a layman means I don't have to be as respectable as a clergyman or as erudite as a theologian. I can say it as it is from the point of view of a real sinner, and a publican to boot, not a trade particularly favoured by the Bible.

CHAPTER ONE

The Circle of Life

I know this is a book about old age but just as I started writing it, I got ambushed by a fetus. It made me think. Death casts a shadow over old age. Death is about nothingness. Conception is about bringing something out of nothing. We enter this world and we depart this world as nothing.

I was standing in a crowd outside St Andrew's Cathedral in Inverness waiting patiently for the do-gooder bearing the Olympic flame to come running round the corner, when I got the phone call. In fact, it was precisely at the moment the torch bearer finally arrived that my mobile phone went off and I heard my precious twenty-five year-old daughter, Angie, completely devoid of a husband, confess to me she was pregnant. A cheer went up from the crowd.

I did not know whether to laugh or to cry. I had been waiting to applaud for about an hour and so I was programmed for a good feeling. The flame arrives, the bomb is dropped. There was silence for a moment.

'You stupid girl!' I eventually bellowed. 'How can this have happened?' OK, not good fathering. 'You've got a degree . . . a 2/1 for God's sake . . . in English!'

Why should the subject matter? I think because it is the polar opposite of science. We all know what scientists are like. Paradoxically enough, they can be scatter-brained when it comes to practical matters and they can overlook the blitheringly obvious like contraception. Also, my point was that Angie was not some damned fool teenage NED (Scottish for non-educated delinquent). She had education. In moments of crisis, unfortunately, you can appear in the full glory and essentials of your own prejudices.

Obviously, as a man I am disqualified from having an opinion about abortion and I had to listen in silence to my daughter saying that it didn't matter. She had booked herself into an abortion clinic for the following Sunday, which I subsequently discovered to be, funnily enough, Father's Day.

The fetus would only be six weeks old and I was told that nowadays there were no horrible invasive scrapings and such like. You just popped a pill.

My sister, Sophia, warned me not to influence my daughter one way or another because if she kept the baby as a result of my advice, she could at some future date blame me for her reduced lifestyle as a single mother.

I had never really thought about abortion before in my life because I had not previously been visited by one of the two classic moral dilemmas: the other being adultery. However, I spent the next three days thinking of nothing else and just for my own benefit even wrote down my arguments, imagining I was putting the case to Angie.

Priests are like philosophers in their distrust of the visible world. Ultimate reality is invisible. Priests say it is spiritual. Whatever it is, you should use your mind like a philosopher, employing language and logic as accurately as possible to understand the reality that underlies appearance.

So you should immediately dismiss the crass but conventional argument that an early fetus is really small and does not look like a person and so it doesn't matter if you get rid of it. An atom is smaller even than a conjoined cell at the moment of conception and yet you split it and you can wipe out a city. So, infinitesimal things can have huge impact.

Instead of approaching the issue visually, you should subject it to the rigours of language and logic.

Linguistically, abortion does not stack up. Everything under the sun, as in the parlour game, is either animal, vegetable or mineral. Angie had called this fetus a lentil. Her analogy is wrong. She would have been more accurate if she had called it a tadpole because her fetus is not a vegetable. And it is obviously not a pebble. At the very moment of conception it became a living being. And what type of being? Well, it was not a dog being or a cat being. A scientist would stick it under an internal microscope, analyse its DNA and come up with a big smile on his face and say triumphantly: 'I tell you what it is, it's a being of the human variety: a human being – be it ever so small.'

So from the point of view of language, there is only one way of describing a fetus from the moment of conception and that is 'a human being'.

Logically, there is a problem as well. Abortionists argue that fetuses gradually become babies like the way children gradually become adults, so you can't kill adults or children or babies but you can kill fetuses. That would be true if the issue was one of maturity rather than essence.

What makes us special is not our intelligence at any given stage of our development because dogs are cleverer than babies but some other quality that is inscribed in our DNA at the moment of conception. Atheists might call that quality, individuality. Religious people call it soul.

Philosophers have a technique for showing up a false argument. It is by reducing it through logic to a statement of absurdity. The method is called *reductio ad absurdum*. As has been already pointed out, the entire case for abortion is based on a gradualist view of the formation of a human being.

As with all wonky thinking, if ever it is implemented, you get hilarious incidents of farce and the case for abortion is no exception. The problem about setting a time limit on abortion is that it makes the whole procedure arbitrary: hence the chronic disagreement between the three leading cultural nations of the Western World as to when precisely that moment is. France has ruled ten weeks, Germany twelve weeks and Britain, a staggering twenty-four weeks.

Do you know what that means? The French in their collective wisdom have decided that a ten-week one moment fetus is human. So, obviously, they think that the Germans and the British have sanctioned programmes of pre-natal murder. And the Germans must think they are twice as bright as us because they think that a German fetus becomes human in half the time we do!

My mother had a miscarriage at twelve weeks and she said it came out recognisably human: arms, legs, head, and a body, so she baptised it herself with water from the tap and then flushed it down the toilet. I think that scene sums up the hard and the gentle of the matter.

The thing is, of course, a fetus is human at 9 weeks, 8 weeks and so on right down to six weeks – the EARLIEST moment you can have an abortion in this country. A six-week fetus has a head for goodness sake. I am sorry, but you cannot kill something with a head. But the abortionists go *head-schmead.* Fetuses up to a certain age don't feel anything and they are not even aware of their own existence. But the same could be said of somebody in a coma, and you would never sanction the termination of a coma patient if the prognosis was that he or she was due to return to consciousness in 9 months.

Of course, as Dostoyevsky said: 'If God doesn't exist, everything is permitted.' You might have a niggle about the potentiality issue as discussed earlier but what the hell; there is no Day of Judgement. Even if abortion is wrong, you don't have to pay for it.

The problem is God. He's the bloody nightmare in this scenario.

The Catholic Church rightly teaches that the soul of a being enters at conception and departs at death. This is, at least, logical because a soul is not something tangible like a brain. It is the youness of you, in my daughter's case, the Angie, blue-printed in her DNA, indelibly formed at the moment of conception. It is the self. It is, of course, invisible. The body is merely its host. It is hardly as if Angieness waited until she reached the age of consent!

If you ask a scientist for an explanation of the phenomenon of conception, he will say that it happens as a result of the sperm of the male piercing the exterior of a female's egg and lodging itself within it.

But the philosopher will then say: 'Yes, that is the visible cause and effect of the start of life but it does not ultimately answer the question of how that biological interaction produces such an effect.'

At that point you have to call in the priest who says it is a mystery. Human life is sacred. Its conception is a miracle and to undo what God has done is a sacrilege. Mind you, there is a massive let out clause, summed up in the words of the Lord: 'Forgive them for they know not what they do.'

That is the strictly rational, unforgiving, male truth of the matter. The intuitive female truth, which is all about the spirit of the thing and is consequently more generous in its deliberation, allows youth and circumstance a certain play and definitely entertains many an exception to the rule such as incidents of rape or incapacitating disability. It also permits the morning after pill on the grounds that destruction of a fleeting embryo of a conjoined cell is more biological interference than theft of a life.

Having formulated my opinion, I desperately tried not to relay it to my daughter. There were three reasons. I was a man. It's her life. I might be wrong. But then I thought: what about the baby? No one was speaking up for the unborn baby. Surely he or she should, at least, have a voice. Just about everybody of Angie's age group was advising her to have the abortion and that it was not a big deal – everybody that is except her boyfriend, Andy, who had only narrowly escaped being aborted himself. His mother had changed her mind about getting rid of him on the very day of her appointment at the abortion clinic. Pity! I couldn't help but think.

Andy's views were typically flip: 'Everybody thinks we would be hopeless parents and we might just smash it. Poppa Fraser will cough up when it comes to the dough and we will get a lie-in on Sunday.' The appointment was 10 in the morning on that Sunday. Angie's mother's advice was just not to go on to the Internet because if she caught sight of an image of a six-week fetus it might upset her.

Then I thought that Angie was a graduate and so was perfectly capable of coming to a rational decision about this issue and did not need to be protected from a dissenting point of view. I was only using logic in defence of the unborn baby and I was merely one voice against the crowd.

What shocked me was that Angie was making an important decision in her life without having taken everything into account. I was amazed at how little she had considered the question, so convinced was she by the case for normality. It was extraordinary that some-body so socially sophisticated could be so undeveloped when it came to moral philosophy. I concluded that these were two totally different areas of expertise and she had only so much time in her frantically busy life.

So we argued on the phone and she cried for four days. I could not help myself once I had started. It was the advocate in me. I really went to town on the poor girl, but everybody else was going: 'Abort! Abort! Abort!'

I went on to make the point that despite current mores, the fact of the matter is that sex was not a double gin and tonic, it was bloody serious stuff. Accidental pregnancies were the proof. If you played with fire, she should expect to get burnt at least once.

Sex was not for children. It was for men and women and quite frankly anybody under the age of twenty-five was a child, which was why they so often behaved so outrageously to one another in their sexual relationships. The ideal, of course, was only to have sex within the confines of marriage but our culture militates against that and I would always be reluctant to try and set an individual up against the power of the group. For most of us it was too big an ask. Angie laughed out loud at this and told me to go back to the Fifties.

Then I talked to Angie about conscience. 'Normally what happens if you want to behave badly is you get your rational mind to justify your behaviour. The one thing, however, you can't fix is your conscience. Intuitively, we know abortion is wrong which is why so many women who have had one, are ashamed of it. They try and keep it a secret.' I said.

Then I was underhand enough to play on her imagination. I said in future years when she eventually did have a family, she would find herself looking at her other children and think: 'I could have aborted you just like the way I aborted your brother or sister.' and look what you have rubbed out – a whole individual person with a unique potential. There is a gap in the family where a character should be.

I said she could defend herself against this possibility by compartmentalising the whole incident of the abortion. She would have to box it off in her brain and slam the door shut on the whole trauma. She would have to desensitise herself which is a large price to pay for peace of mind. However, if she was unlucky enough not to have children for some reason or other and there is no guaranteeing the little nippers, she could be as rational as she liked but a horrible little voice deep inside her would attribute the failure to the earlier fatal decision. 'You are only human and there is no stilling the quite inner voice.' Lots of women suffer for years after their abortions.

Angie said she had several friends who had had abortions at six weeks. It was just a question of popping a pill and being sick for three days. Pregnancy would make you sick for three months and, furthermore, they said they had not regretted their decision in the slightest.

I then played another dirty trick. I call it the David versus Goliath manoeuvre. Nobody wants to be Goliath. I said she was up against the cultural norm and how could she as a lone, and now suddenly particularly vulnerable, individual be expected to think for herself when the soundings of her solitary little mind were being drowned out by the chorus of opinion that clamoured for her to take the easy option. Her weaker self, encouraged by the group mentality, was being asked to give in to itself. It was a formidable alliance – the tough decision being disapproved of by her peer group. Fellow countrymen in Czechoslovakia were delighted when the hero in Milan Kundera's *The Unbearable Lightness of Being* gave in to the secret police because it made everybody else, who had colluded with the State, feel better about themselves.

Who would not succumb to such an opposition? Angie was lucky, I said. At least she had a Desperate Dad putting an alternative view. At least she had a choice. I then said: 'Shit comes in two forms: concrete and liquid.'

'What do you mean? Diarrhoea?'

I ignored her flippant response, I was being deadly serious. 'Shit happens to everybody. Liquid or diarrhoea as you call it, I see as low level boredom, dissatisfaction and frustration. Concrete, or solids as you might put it, is any disastrous event. And I will agree, you getting pregnant is crap.

'The making of a person happens in how they respond to shit in whatever form it appears. Rowena is eighteen with an accidental baby to a far from ideal, chance boyfriend in the Australian outback. If she responds positively to her temporary nightmare, and temporary can be a decade, she will reappear in the UK at the age of thirty a very impressive woman.'

Rowena was the younger sister of a childhood friend of Angie's and she had got herself pregnant on her gap year. She decided to have the baby as a result of which she was not allowed out of Australia with her offspring until it was twelve years old, without her boyfriend's consent because he was half Aborigine. It was Australian law.

I concluded by saying that abortion would affect her view of herself because she would have to accommodate that dreadful decision. She would have to see herself as necessarily tough and sensible and practical. I think that would mean a narrowing of the mental arteries that go from your heart to your head. Life from then on would have to be conducted in prose. She might miss the poetry.

Then I played the lowest card of the lot – the two of clubs. Having the abortion was the sensible option, I said, or at least appeared to be. Having the baby was heroic.

I tell you, that baby made it by a whisker.

It was the indecision that had made Angie cry. Once she had made up her mind to have the baby, she felt much better. Everyone was very tactful as they are in these cases and there were lots of notional pledges of support for her brave decision, although obviously I came in for a certain amount of criticism for having interfered in my daughter's life and for having sacrificed her personal freedom on the altar of my fierce Christian rectitude. You can't be criticised for doing and saying nothing, which makes that such an attractive option.

What made me feel better about the whole affair was what my sister, Sophia, told me Angie had told her. Angie had said she knew that if she told me about the pregnancy she would be having the baby by Christmas. She finally told me a week before the appointment with the clinic, so deep within her she had obviously already made up her mind. She just needed me for confirmation.

Seven and a half months later she had the baby. This is my diary entry:

> The new baby was born at 2 am. Angie phoned at 8 am. saying she couldn't get it to stop crying. I said they are less trouble in than out.

My restaurant staff, who naturally do not believe in God but believe in the stars instead, had told me that the most important moment in my grandchild's life would be the moment of his birth because that would determine the whole of his life. It was all in the stars, they said. For your information, he is Pisces but I intend to have him brought up Roman Catholic.

Anyway all this talk of stars did get me looking up at the heavens last night when I heard that Angie had started labour and I was amazed to see a rainbow round the moon. I then went to my friend and bookkeeper, Mary Quinn's, for supper and saw it again outside her house and so asked her to come out and have a look at it but she couldn't see it. I said she must be short-sighted. It was a large rainbow going right round the moon, starting at the nearest star to it. No, she couldn't see a thing and neither could three passers-by whom we stopped and asked whether they could see this circular rainbow. I then told Mary to get a pen and paper and write down the colours of the rainbow working from the outermost ring. How could I be hallucinating a rainbow when I was accurately describing the colours?

I stayed overnight at Mary Quin's so I could drink as much as I liked over dinner. During the course of the night I was woken up by one of her cats sounding like a baby, crying as only a cat can. It was a sign that the baby had been born and I looked at my mobile phone and, sure enough, there was the glorious text: 'Baby born'.

In the morning another friend, Leonie, texted asking me whether the baby was born and I texted: 'Yes' and then she texted: 'What was the baby going to call you?' I texted: 'Grandpa Chiefy' (My childhood nickname was 'Chiefy') but at the first attempt the predictive text was 'Church'. At the second attempt, the predictive text was 'Christ'.

Obviously this is a special baby destined for a religious life and being a Fraser, wildly ambitious. So there is only one job for him. I think we are looking at the birth of the first mixed race Pope: Pope Barrack the First!'

*

I forgot to mention, his father is half Nigerian. The Papacy had been on my mind because this was during the brief period when one Pope had resigned and the next one had not been elected, so there was a vacancy.

When I first clapped my eyes on the infant child, I did a double take because I have never seen a baby look more like a little Pope. His head was cone-shaped, perfectly adapted for the Papal headgear. No mitre had a keener fit. You could slip it on and it would not blow away in a cross wind.

'O Ange,' I said. 'I love its little papal feet.'

Angie was worried it was breathing too fast and I reassured her that all babies breathe fast. I said: 'You are born a fast breather and as you get older you breathe more and more slowly until eventually you stop breathing altogether.' The district nurse came in and declared an emergency. She said the baby was breathing at twice the normal rate and needed to be taken to hospital immediately. It was nothing too much to worry about. It had an immaturity in its respiratory system and the solution was to feed it up so that it concluded this final stage in its development as quickly as possible. The hospital doctors said the solution was to starve it so the baby was denied food for four days until it was in so much distress even they relented. Then the breathing problem mysteriously resolved itself. It came out of hospital after ten days and embarked on life in civvy street.

Back in the flat I looked at the baby and I thought that it looked as helpless as my other sister, Arabella, in the last few days of her life – with a big round face – hers was blown up with steroids as part of her treatment for cancer – incapable of speech, mostly sleeping, waited on hand and foot by her mother, surrounded by members of the family, soothed merely by their presence, reduced to being fed in liquid form and we sang lullabies. One was leaving and the other was entering this world. I don't think life is a straight line with a beginning and an end. I think it's a circle.

O reader, I would like to apologise for having had the audacity to broach the subject of abortion considering my sex but, the other end of life, old age – the subject of my book – is all about the prospect of non-existence.

I know I have to tread carefully. I have already trod on the toes of one of the readers of the manuscript of this book, outraged that I had 'sacrificed my grandson on the altar of my rectitude'.

'What,' he said, 'do you think he will feel in later life about his mother for having even considered aborting him?'

'But having decided against it,' I said, 'I expect him to feel great pride and eternal gratitude for having stood up to the chorus of opinion of her friends pleading with her to take the sensible decision. That is how his father, Andy, feels about his mother who took the same decision in identical circumstances.'

'But who says the son will react the same way as the father?'

'Genetics, upbringing and free will,' I said, 'Nature, Nurture and Nietzsche.'

And the mother: how does she feel, having taken that irreversible decision?

Well, let me refer to the law, still current today, which says that a doctor can only carry out an abortion if he first signs a form stating that in his professional opinion the patient would otherwise suffer from mental illness. I assume they mean depression rather than actual madness. The only visible effect that I can detect in Angie in the first few months since the birth of her baby has been, for want of a better word, Joy.

CHAPTER TWO

Elixir

Carpe diem before diem carpes you. That should be your motto when you enter old age and 60 is the date of entry. When you stepped out of school or university you had your teenage dreams of doing good for others, individually or in general, or else maybe you harboured ambitions to become a world beater in some art form.

Listen to the comedian Jack Dee's observation on his first job as a waiter in a pizza restaurant chain when he was being considered for management. His cathartic moment occurred at a meeting to decide how many pieces of pineapple topping should be included in a new Hawaiian pizza. 'I had become aware,' he said, 'that all the other waiters had something else they were doing in their lives – drama students had a band, performing poetry. And I didn't. But I felt I belonged to them much more than to this group of pizza managers. I just thought this is my life and I am talking about pieces of pineapple.'

The dream of freedom worked for Jack Dee because he had more than just a little talent but for the rest of us realism kicks in midway through our twenties and we realise we are doomed to live our working life at the beck and call of others, slaves to the treadmill of the 40 hour (9–5) week, minimum, which allows us the weekend to give enough time to recover for Monday.

But now you are stepping out again into the world for the second time. Only this time you are free to do whatever you want. You have got a pension and only yourself to spend it on and the one thing that a pension can buy is the most valuable commodity of all time: time. Time to go back to the point at which you left off, in your twenties – when you had to abandon your dreams of self-expression. O Callooh! Callay! What a wonderful day!

Of course, there are those of you who have given up. You cannot resuscitate yourselves because in my view you have come to the wrong conclusions about life. Your intervening years between youth and old age have taught you the wrong things. You have taken the Amis route.

Either life is a game and ultimately has no meaning or it is serious. Some of us live in a post mortem society in which the spirit of man, nurtured and celebrated in religion, is neglected in favour of various forms of death: nihilism, anarchism, cynicism, hedonism, materialism, pessimism, existentialism, agnosticism, alcoholism and atheism.

Martin Amis has an obsession with sex and his father, Kingsley, had one with alcohol and they both have a mutual interest in bodily functions. Their linguistically brilliant and hilarious books are about the body because for them the soul does not exist. The most profound thing Kingsley can say about life is that nice things are nicer than nasty. They make no distinction between big and little. Their attitude is the stuff of modern literary criticism which does not prioritise Shakespeare over a telephone directory – just two different texts, and the telephone directory is more interesting than Hamlet if what you want is a phone number.

The Amises are entirely logical. Without God, morality does not exist. It is just something foisted on you by society to keep you in order. Philosophy is just pretentious crap. Their heroes, or anti-heroes, are admired for playing the game of life with panache.

To be called a player is the ultimate accolade in the city where those suited and booted bastards gamble with the nation's finances. The original Rothschild, a pillar, if ever there was one, of the city establishment, is much admired by financiers the world over for having made millions during the Napoleonic wars. He misled rival investors about the result of the Battle of Waterloo, causing a collapse in the stock market whereupon he secretly set about buying up millions of shares. That is the culture of money.

Money is a means to an end, and the end is happiness. The convention, of course, is that you cannot buy it, although one thing we know for sure is that a dire shortage of money can make you unhappy. Having said that, I went to Africa and I have never seen so many happy people and such grinding poverty. To me it was concrete proof that happiness is spiritual. The spirit is infinite.

A finite fellow is somebody who believes by the time you are adult you basically know the fundamentals of life. To all intents and purposes you have reached the end of knowledge. Any more learning will just bring you more information, and so, philo-sophically speaking, you have given up. Apparently the average child asks 356 questions a day, but that does include 87 'whys?' Now suddenly you have stopped. Ted Hughes once told me that most people stop at the age of sixteen. 'That is when most peoples' minds close down,' he said. Pope Benedict had some important things to say on his visit to Britain but he sadly realised that he could only talk to people who were capable of listening. He defined them as 'those who are seeking answers to the fundamental questions of life.' To me that's the definition of life. If you are not doing that, you are just treading water.

Going drinking with a finite fellow is formulaic. You will never get to that magic point in the evening when your inhibitions are gone and both your minds are wide open and you are prepared to consider any proposition. Anything is possible.

A finite fellow believes in a variety of style but the content is fixed. It is quite a problem marrying one of these people because you can very quickly get to the end of their conversation and once the children have gone and you enter old age, what is there left to distract you? The solution, they attempt, is movement. So you manically fill your lives with different people and places.

I remember a great line in a book that haunted me with reason. It said enough happened to this fellow in a week to provide him with enough conversation to make him entertaining at a dinner party as long as he was gone by midnight. I can't for the life of me remember the name of the book but I do remember the line. The problem about old age is that movement eventually slows down to the point of stillness.

Being literary geniuses, the Amises have total integrity. They are always honest. They tell the truth from their perspective. What they realise time and again in their books is that pure atheism, taken to its logical conclusion, makes you unhappy. If life is only a game, as they advocate, and all you do is play it no matter how entertainingly, it will make you desperate. Let me just quote you three lines from Martin Amis's *London Fields*.

First, a little bit of background. His chief male protagonist, Keith Talent, is trying to win a darts competition and his female lead, Nicola Six, is trying to get herself killed in the most original way she can imagine. Amis's authorial message is that even death is a game and darts are as important or unimportant as love.

Occasionally he interrupts his litany of jokes, his panoply of post-modern irony, his heavy kitsch, his verbal fireworks, his astounding purple passages describing modern life, to make a plain statement direct from him to the reader about the human condition as he sees it. 'And besides, he was completely desperate, as many of us are these days.' And: 'We are most of us,' I said, 'in some kind of agony.' And: 'that song: such complication, such grievous entanglement. First, you go through this, it was saying. Then you go through this. Life, thought Guy.' And finally, the author describes some old ladies like this: 'All of them had been adored and wept over, presumably, at one point, prayed to, genuflected in front of, stroked, kissed, licked and now the bald unanimity of disappointment, of compound grief and grievance.'

If that is where atheism takes you, I prefer, if I possibly can, to believe in God. If that is where exclusive gamesmanship takes you, I prefer to mix purpose with my play. If that is the way of the world, I will, at least, seek the life of the spirit.

There is a right way to give up as you enter old age and that is to give up on projection and just be yourself as you should be. Old age is an opportunity to rejoin the human race and live it again like you did last summer or rather the last summer you really felt you were living – which was probably the last summer before employment. You don't have to pretend to be a doctor or a businessman or an expert of any sort any more. You can say things like: 'I haven't got a clue.' Or: 'I might well be wrong, in fact I probably am, indeed I can look back on my life and it has been a catalogue of mistakes which is why what you see before you is a penniless divorceeeeee – yes you can count every one of those 'e's, there's lots of them.' Or else you can say with some confidence: 'I am a smug and successful buffooooooon. Just wallow in those 'o's. I have 100 acquaintances and no real friends at all but, and here is the very big BUT – I have now got a good twenty years to become human again in the full sense of the word. I am no longer answerable to society at large or some fat bastard at work, who for some reason, unbeknownst to me, has just been promoted over my head so that he personally can make my life, if not miserable, certainly frustrating.'

'No one is here by accident. Each one of us was sent here for a special destiny,' writes John O'Donohue, the author of the spiritual masterpiece and global bestseller, *Anam Cara*. 'You were sent a shape of destiny in which you would be able to express the special gift you bring to the world.'

What is your destiny? What is your gift? You will be able to sum yourself up in a word. Aim for that word these last twenty years. I was one of four people who gave a eulogy at my sister Arabella's memorial service. I ended it with the words: 'I think everybody in their lives has some special thing to contribute to the developing culture of a family. Each person can be summed up in one word which encapsulates their lives and the reason they are put on this Earth. We have lost six women in our family. Aunt Anne whose word, I think, is style. Aunt Ibi – endurance, Aunt Jenny – chat,

Aunt Fanny – love, Kate Rous – gumption and Arabella – serenity.'

Incidentally, I have worked out my own epitaph: 'I tried. I cried. I died.' Try-ers are supposed to be loved by God and on that hook I hang my hat. But I won't have done it by myself. I will have had help from my three best friends: Alcohol, Television and God Himself.

Like all good friends, I fall out with them on occasion. Sometimes I get bored of Television. Months can go by when I don't really make contact with God. He just sort of disappears and I can argue with Alcohol. Sometimes I really disagree with him or rather he disagrees with me, but one way or another, I always come back to him, normally at a party and then O God it is good to be back on that emotional roller-coaster again! Part of my problem is that my three friends don't get on with one another. I have to see them separately.

You might be surprised at my choice of friends to accompany me through old age. I call them my Trinity: three in one and one in three. I don't want to be sacrilegious but I see my friend God as an authority figure – God the Father; television as God the Son because television is myriad in its talent, omniscient in its knowledge of the world in all its complexity and above all, friendly. Television is never patronising. It's in the soup with you, empathetic to the last degree and oh does it do suffering! And Drink is God the Holy Ghost. Drink is like prayer. It has the same effect on your spirit, but gentler. It temporarily lifts your spirit and makes you feel human again – as you should be.

People think it is sad when I tell them who my best friends are. They think it means that I am not only lonely but also that I have given up trying to be a part of the life that surrounds me. They are worried I will become a recluse. Not a bit of it. Television for me is shorthand for knowledge. By television, I mean the internet as well and indeed all media for information and entertainment, so that includes journalism and literature and film: fiction and non-fiction. So God the Son feeds my intellect and God the Holy Ghost gets me out at night in search of company to share a bottle. God the Holy

28

Ghost fills pubs and restaurants. He breathes life into a community. It is why Jesus Christ turned his blood into wine rather than Ribena.

God the Father is just the object of my prayers. Between the three of them they give me the sustenance to take on the world and form temporary alliances with people who, given time, can in turn, become friends, although not as reliable as my three best friends who will never desert me, who are there when everybody else is otherwise occupied, whom I can call up at the touch of a button, the pop of a cork or the sign of a cross.

On a less grandiose level there are sometimes days in old age when you are not due to see anybody. A day like that you have to attack the moment you crack your eyes open in the morning in bed. You have to defeat that sinking feeling in the pit of your stomach. Bang! Down on your knees! 30 minutes of prayer. Nipped you in the bud, you bastard! Now what's for breakfast?

The morning is for reading a book or going for a walk and buying a newspaper. Lunch has to be the pub. Obviously, you never want to drop below the government weekly recommended limit for a male adult which is 21 units. That is 10 pints of beer, one and a half pints a day, seven days a week. It is quite a punishing schedule but these pubs need filling. Currently 10 of them are closing a week and I am sure there is some link between that awful depressing statistic and Margaret Thatcher's observation that there is no such thing as society any more. This has to be overturned and as the old battle-axe herself said: 'Decline is not inevitable.' You must just go out there and drink and where there's drink there's talk.

Back home for a light nap. The afternoon is for writing old-fashioned letters and sliding them into V-backed envelopes, addressed, stamped and posted. Receiving a personal, hand-written letter is better than opening a Christmas present. It is as complimentary as a prayer said by somebody on your behalf. Night time on these dud days obviously is for television. When you look to the heavens to get you through a blank evening, it's good to have Sky.

CHAPTER THREE

Decline and Fall

As you topple into old age, you gradually become aware of a reduction of self. You have moments of realisation which reflect badly on you.

The whole battery of psychologists emphasises the importance of self-esteem. So you spend your whole, active, conscious, working life trying to increase your personal power.

Everybody has got a private self-improvement programme which runs alongside their work schedule. The fruits of that dual effort should be displayed for all to admire and you to enjoy. There should be wife, kids, friends, house, cash – but the problem is that just at the moment when you have finally got the time to really concentrate on everybody, divorce (which affects damn near half of us) puts paid to the entire retirement plan.

Maybe I'm an extreme example. My current crib is rented. All the property I used to own has gone west to pay for my divorce. I am wheeled out for high days and holidays to view the kids, who are too busy trying to make their own way in the world. So I have just got my so-called friends to concentrate on. In that respect, as a self-employed entrepreneur, I am luckier than a lot of people who on retirement lose all their friends at work. Bankruptcy is my retirement.

Still, how do I maintain my all-important self-esteem when I have been to a certain extent abandoned by my nearest and dearest *and* due to the ageing process, find myself personally on the slide?

I fall asleep during the day at least once – quite frankly, if ever I am left alone in the afternoon. Boff . . . I'm away like a toddler in a car.

My brain, which I have consciously spent my life trying to improve, is very occasional. I can't rely on it, which makes life exceedingly precarious because I never know when it is going to go on the blink. It can rise to the occasion or stubbornly refuse. And there's one thing we do know about the brain. You can't just tell it do stuff. It has got to feel like it, and as I get older I am noticing it feels like it less and less.

I never did have a good memory which is a big reason why I have so religiously kept diaries since the age of twenty-six but that faculty has certainly deteriorated and I think I can, with some confidence, put that down to drink. I have not entirely wasted my time as a restaurant owner and publican of 30 years standing.

Names obstinately refuse to attach themselves to faces. I have reached the stage of blissful ignorance perfected by my late father who loved to hear stories that he had heard before because he could not remember a word of them, but they stirred within him a vague feeling of nostalgia and a promise of happy endings.

My energy levels are way down and there is no guarantee that whenever I go to bed with anybody, my willy won't go wonky. God is a practical joker, don't you find? When you can't get anywhere near a girl due to gross incompetence and a sort of blanket incomprehension of all things female in your late teens, your penis is jumping up and down like a yoyo. Then gifted bachelorhood in your late fifties, thanks to an erring wife, you are now receiving attention from a fantastic crop of divorced women who are finally interested in the nice guys, and suddenly the penis gets all moody.

The other terrifying thing is that I find myself being outstripped by the up and coming generations. I have always thought of myself as a funny fellow. I have comforted myself with that thought. I might be a failure but at least I'm funny. It is the classic British default position.

But now modern life, which suits humour, has bred new generations of really fast and witty mental athletes and my ponderous labouring anecdotes are left gasping for breath in their wake. You only have to compare today's stand-up comedians to people like Ken Dodd, Tommy Cooper or Morecambe and Wise, the best of our crop, to see how far comedy has come since my youth, which is when you form your sense of humour to last you a lifetime.

And also you seem to solidify as you get older and you become shy of young peoples' social mobility, their brilliant flexibility, the way they can all bundle into the back of a van and drive away on holiday and come back and say: 'What an amazing time we had!'

What can happen as you get older, especially if you are a careerist in your work, is that distance increases between you and other people until you become more of a spectator than a participant and eventually, if you are not careful: a solitary individual with your nose perpetually pressed up against the window looking in at a happy party.

Do you want to end up like John Fowles' wife? He was the celebrated author who wrote the book behind the film, *The French Lieutenant's Woman*. In later life he confided to his diary: 'Talk after talk with Eliza in London over the telephone, listening to her absorption in her misery over the flat in Pembridge Crescent . . . her misery over her identity, who she is, do I love her, does anyone love her, her isolation.'

You get one chance to break the hardening mould that forms like a carapace around your eager heart, and that is your mid-life crisis, but here in old age I am offering another chance to have a break-down! Yippee!

One's mind can have silted up. We all know why. The company, or the sequence of companies, for whom you have worked for your entire life, has bought your brain and now they have returned it to you on the day of your retirement – not only has it become a slave of routine, it can't bear freedom, any freedom. It is scared of the chaos of youth, the anarchic ribaldry of the working-class and, of course, an aristocrat is just a black hole of amorality into which you would disappear leaving no trace of your former well-behaved self – money and style providing the necessary cover so that to the eye of the outsider, everything looks quite normal and as it should be.

And the other problem is that too much time by yourself actually makes you intolerant of other people, thus compounding your solitude. One weekend, a couple of years ago, I had to brace myself for a little invasion. There I was in my rented cottage and my quiet home life consisted of padding from kitchen to living room and back again according to whether I wanted food or entertainment. Now suddenly I was obliged to put up a couple of guests for the weekend. They were up from England to attend my sister's funeral. Arek and Teddy are just a pair of standard male egotists not noted for their awareness of other people so interested are they in what they are saying – great in small doses. This is my diary entry for what happened at the end of the weekend:

> Outburst occurred after two and a half days of being nice to people on a continuous basis no matter who next comes through the door. Unnaturally cheerful minute by minute for the guts of 56 hours sometimes without the aid of booze and only brief intervals of sleep tests my tolerance levels.

The reason we have a thing called the weekend is that it bloody ends, thank goodness, but it feels like a week. It has been worked out by society that a weekend is as long as it takes for homo sapiens, especially the male of the species, to want to start killing his neighbour with whom he has been so unnaturally closeted within the confines of a house and, as such, as a guest you are taking your life in your hands if you have failed to leave on Sunday afternoon as required. Woe-betide the guest who turns up all chipper for Monday breakfast! And two of them are doubling the danger.

Arek and Teddy had been talking their heads off at one another for the half hour it took me to prepare our breakfast. Three boiled eggs were finally in place ready for decapitation and I, as the expression goes, 'went off on one'. Lid having been blown, apologies all round – Catholic guilt in the ascendant.

The camel-back-breaking feather was Arek having just given me a ten-minute lecture on a business idea I had recommended to somebody, finally asked me a question only to interrupt my reply. That is all he did. But I had not been able to get a word in edgeways between these two guests of mine one way and another all weekend. Why should that matter when my own sister had just been buried? I don't know. It just did.

'Here's a little tip: Don't ask a question.' I shouted, rage flooding through me like heroin. 'Don't even ask if you're not going to allow a reply! It's a total imposition! And I'm not having it! So you can fuck off! And so can you! You can both fuck off! You can finish your breakfast which I have been bloody well preparing for you while you have just gassed on as if I don't exist! Just fuck off the pair of you!'

Arek stormed out of the room in a towering rage himself at having been shouted at by his erstwhile host. 'I don't suppose I could have his egg.' said Teddy.

And let's not talk about my body. The effect of the ageing process on the body is something I don't intend to explore except to say that I am grateful I am not a woman. Men are visual, no matter how much feminists would wish it otherwise, and a lot of woman's power comes from her looks and it's a rare sixty year old – or more likely a fake one – who has managed to retain a fraction of the allure she will have enjoyed in her heyday.

Actually, the body fares relatively well compared to the face and ultimately it is the face that concentrates our attention. A good face can carry a lot of crap body. Apparently the nose never stops growing, which is another of God's little jokes, and so as you grow old you gradually get out of proportion. The colour scheme goes haywire as you redden up and go grey at the edges and then comes

The March of the Wrinkles. Obviously, women fight a rear guard action with a whole palette of make-up and selection of hair dyes, but there is the harsh light of the morning which can put pay to the most promising of late night entanglements. No, second marriages are for the short-sighted.

Or else, as a fellow, you drop down a generation and have your self-confidence gradually eroded as your paramour imperceptibly comes into herself while you are on the way out and the balance of power, which determines all relationships, goes against you.

Nothing works like it used to and there's a reason for that. Purpose recedes with age. The old imperatives have subsided. You no longer have to provide for your family. Your mortgage has been paid off and anyway there's no work to go to because you have been put out to grass, as if you are a cow and, like a cow, you have got to learn to eat grass all day long without getting bored.

In what you now regard as the good old days, although they certainly did not feel like that at the time, happiness, or at least contentment, started for you and millions like you, with a boiled egg at breakfast and a nice hot steaming cup of coffee, then a good day at work where you practised your expertise, chatted with friends and then came home to a basically loving wife, an assortment of children, a couple of stiff drinks, nice nosh, telly, bed and sex if you're lucky.

Existential angst, a need for a higher purpose, anything deep and meaningful, the whole notion of God, for example, is foreign territory to the vast majority of young and middle-aged people in the UK. We now have the perfect balance of ease and distraction mostly at the touch of a button. We can dispense with politics, religion and philosophy. Who needs big when little is so entertaining? The only problem is old age when silence comes pouring into our lives.

CHAPTER FOUR

Is that it?

Success, which made you feel great – that is, if you were lucky enough to have achieved it – no longer does the job. The problem is that a lifetime of single-minded pursuit of it has done irretrievable damage to you which only now becomes apparent in old age when the merry-go-round of chase-the-pound-note has ground to a halt.

Success is particularly hard for secular people. They take the things of this world so seriously because for them this is the only world. Of course, a lifetime of deadly seriousness does not prepare you for old age, when you have as much time as you had as a student, with as little to do, and so what is required now is a totally different set of skills: Playfulness being the most desired attribute of the aged.

I had an interesting conversation with my niece, Vanessa, about her friend, Turina, who is anything but successful. It was in the context of a discussion we were having about the self and the brain. Vanessa made the excellent point that driven people, high achievers, who allow self too much control over their brain can easily become effective, but ultimately boring. Unlike her friend, Turina, who allows her brain free reign. She is highly entertaining but has no self-control and she is prone to depression. She recently went through what she called her 'Blue Period' when she spent most of the day in water, or in the bathroom to be precise. 'She became distinctly aquatic,' said Vanessa.

Turina's parents had both died, leaving her to be looked after by her horrible uncle and aunt who used her inheritance to take her on exotic holidays.

What's fun about Turina are her fads and the way she is so

energetic in her pursuit of fun. She is ready to join clubs, go to parties and help set up things for other people as long as there is promise of action. Turina is all or nothing. 'The problem is she pours her energy into her current boyfriend and so finds herself friendless at the end of the relationship. That is when I get a call up' said Vanessa.

I replied that a lot of books and films have an over-educated narrator desperately trying to shake off the stranglehold of self being initially bowled over by these desperate freedom fighters, people like Turina, highly entertaining chaos warriors whose wacky brains have been allowed to career out of control, creating hilarious situations and first class craic, making in the process, excellent copy for the budding author.

There is of course, some hellish reckoning at the end of the book when the freedom fighter comes a cropper in some form or another and the narrator is left with a huge feeling of nostalgia which he passes on to us, the readers. Total narcotic . . . I am thinking of Scott Fitzgerald's love of his crazy wife Zelda, whom he replicates in all his books; Evelyn Waugh's narrator's love for the doomed Sebastian; Holly Golightly in *Breakfast at Tiffanys*, the Sally Bowles of *Cabaret*, the hero of *One Flew Over The Cuckoo's Nest* and the guys in Jack Kerouac's *On The Road* are all characters of this type with besotted, self-lacerating narrators telling the stories of their tragic heroes and heroines (who are always frightfully good-looking for some odd reason).

Old age for aristocrats is just more of the same and they are masters of play. Their problem is dissolution. By the time they get to their sixties, they tend to run out of steam due to lack of interest. I went on holiday with a group of what I call macro toffs – super toffs without the inherited millions – and so they have been forced to enter the world of work and I thought maybe they had got the magic mix. Of course, as you would expect, they very quickly become successful because of their contacts and their superb genetics, which has gifted them effortless brains and lordly looks. They are all over six foot. Their wives are mostly leisured ladies who, if they do any work, dabble.

I was interested to see how my brother-in-law was such a social success with them. Dave, who describes himself as having come out of 'the sock drawer of the social chest of drawers' has become in middle-age a three-dimensional character, bonded to matter, a man of genuine rhythm, at ease with himself. That is certainly how he looked amongst a pantomime of super toffs with verbal diarrhoea, trained over 10,000 dinner parties and hundreds of weekend house parties never to let a silence fall.

One of the holiday guests, Sophie Somebody-or-other said her family of four super toff sisters needed the calming and solid effect of her engineer husband's presence to give them ballast. Left to themselves they became hysterical, like headless chickens. It reminded me of Paula Yates who said how she loved the company of athletes and sportsmen for their calmness.

There is something solid about Dave, who works with his hands and uses his muscles on a daily basis, with his dogs, his horses and his micro-beer business, whereas all these other guys on that holiday have spent their lives being charming to one another and exploiting other people further down the food chain – all done professionally with the full approval of the Establishment.

They have great manners and are masters of small talk, all conducted with an air of permanent gentle amusement. It makes you want to scream. What really turn them on are money, power, sex and expensive treats in beautiful surroundings. Not a single moment of intensity. They have been groomed since birth and they rule the world. Is that the worm of envy turning in its manure?

My only consolation is that old age will sort them out. Actually, they will probably just go into a graceful and gentle decline, like Britain under Harold Macmillan, while saying they have never had it so good.

Fame is Just a Feeling

But if success is difficult to get right, fame is impossible. I saw a terribly sad documentary on the television about Shirley Bassey. At one point you see her at the top of a table, seating a dozen of her so-called friends in a restaurant. Everyone was pandering to her ego. It was all cheap adolescent buzzes to do with flirting and sexual innuendo. The woman must have been in her late sixties. Instead of a number of conversations up and down the table, it all centred around her. Nobody was enjoying themselves. They were just waiting to leave so they could boast about it to their real friends. You just thought: what a waste of a fabulous woman, hooked on attention and divorced from social reality – too high a personal price for public success but with her talent, she had no choice.

What is the reason why some people who apparently have everything are unhappy? I suppose Brad Pitt, who has probably got more of what the world wants than anybody, summed it up most succinctly when he said: 'Once you have got everything, you find yourself alone.'

'The price of fame,' says pop star, Rick Astley, 'is privacy and friends,' which he did not think was a fair swap so he gave up his singing career only to come back to it a decade later when he was relatively unknown again.

The other downside of fame is that it makes you self-obsessed. Pop star Robbie Williams admitted in the rock doc *Somebody Nobody* that he could not think of anything to say except about himself.

'Receiving deference, paeans and plaudits is addictive, public adulation a fix that has to be repeated. Such a man becomes more and more in love with himself and has less and less warmth to bestow on anybody else. Friendships to him become shallow and are only tolerated as long as they are of any use to him,' wrote Margaret Cook on her ex-husband, Robin Cook, the Labour party foreign secretary under Tony Blair.

The world made Marilyn Monroe so unhappy she killed herself and yet the world could not have been kinder to her. God gave her beauty, sexiness, charm and talent and we gave her wealth and fame. What more could you want? How could she not be happy with all that attention? How could she not be happy with everybody falling over themselves to be her friend and queuing up to make love to her? She was great at her job and she had the best job in the world. Come on, acting is a lot of fun. It is art without the sweat. Even children can do it.

She felt insignificant. She was self-obsessed. Towards the end she had four hour daily sessions with her psychotherapist. She had a great fear of solitude. She was chronically anxious to please but invariably kept people waiting on set. She had no friends. She was pathologically shy and yet she was a public figure. She was described as a delightful guileless child and yet she was a sexual omnivore while not much liking the act of sex because she had difficulties reaching orgasm. She suffered from chronic insomnia. She felt inarticulate. She craved love and attention. She was a compulsive flirt. She could not rid herself of a terrible feeling of emptiness. Acting made her sick with fear. She never went to college but read and reread the works of Rilke, Faulkner and Steinbeck. She thought that for her the only way of being some-body was to pretend to be someone else. She was afraid of becoming mad. She suffered from depression. She had a fear of ageing.

And yet the world with all its ingenuity, including massive amounts of psychotherapy, could give her no comfort.

I am amazed Marilyn Monroe never tried God. He seemed to have worked for Nixon at his worst moment. Henry Kissinger, the Nobel peace prize-winner and statesman, said the greatest moment in his public life was on the day of Nixon's historic resignation as President as a result of the Watergate scandal when just before leaving the Oval Office for the last time, Nixon turned to Kissinger and asked him to kneel down and pray with him. If God does not exist, Kissinger's biggest moment was pure tomfoolery.

Also compare Marilyn Monroe's story to that of Larry Hagman, the globally known US TV star who famously acted JR in *Dallas*. Hell-raiser, as the tabloids call famous actors who love to drink and party, he might have been but he managed the almost impossible feat in the acting profession, let alone Hollywood itself, of remaining happily married to his wife right until death did him part. What was his secret? He spent one day a week alone in silence.

And, what's more, you don't even have to be successful to get into the wrong habits of mind. Just think of all those bureaucrats who make life impossible for the country's 4 million small businessmen who are trying to actually create prosperity to pay for the bureaucrats in the first place. I wouldn't mind government officials if only they were not so missionary-like. There is nothing more pious than a secular man with a book of rules and regulations. He has finally got his Bible.

On a miniature scale, I was stopped by a policeman the other day for having committed the heinous crime of not having dipped my lights when his car came the opposite way in the dark. If he had any sense of perspective, he should have tapped me on the window and said: 'Tiny little thing. Hardly worth stopping you for but technically not dipping your lights to oncoming traffic at night is a motoring offence. It is discretionary as to whether I administer you a fine but, obviously, I will let you off with a caution and incidentally thanks for my wages.'

I don't know why the police have to be so disapproving and if you are not immediately subservient, they become aggressive. This fellow was half my age and treated me like I was an erring schoolboy. The stupid arsehole could not tell the difference between big and little and completely failed to realise, as a civil servant, his job is to serve us the taxpayer and the least we should expect from him is civility. It is not surprising that policemen rarely make happy old men and they never, in my personal experience, make old men happy!

The Best Sex is the Worst

Apart from money, the other great thing the world offers is sex but to really enjoy that to its fullest and most varied extent, you need to dispense with morality. With the best willy in the world, shagging the same woman for thirty or forty years is going to become repetitive. 'Decent men don't badger their wives of twenty years for sexual satisfaction,' advises the adulterer Marvin Kraitman to his uxorious friend, Charlie, in Howard Jacobson's brilliant book about adultery *Who's Sorry Now?*

Nobody said adultery was not massive fun. You are no longer ignorant teenagers jumping into bed because you have run out of conversation. And what happens when you get into bed benefits from the expertise you have picked up along the way. Danger is an aphrodisiac and there is precious little of it in our modern cosseted world where health and safety barely allows you to run in the street. Adultery is real cloak and dagger stuff with huge financial risks, let alone the potential emotional fall-out: sacrificing your nearest and dearest for your darling. I have been advised by an aficionado of that particular lifestyle choice that adultery is very seedy and highly addictive.

Unfortunately there is no such thing as a free lunch and I told my ex-wife exactly that. I said: 'There's no such thing as a free lunch and there will come a day when you will have to pay the bill. I was offered lunch often while we were married but I always turned it down.'

'Well, you are free to have some lunch now. Look on the bright side.'

'I don't want any fucking lunch!'

'Suit yourself but you can actually have lunch now and, so to speak, not pay for it. My adultery has freed you up, lunch-wise.'

'I'm not hungry.'

Roy, the owner of Mailboxes in Station Square in Inverness, told me a story of his best friend at school who was serially adulterous throughout his marriage even to the extent of chasing the bridesmaids at his own wedding. 'It's the thrill of it,' he confided to Roy. 'There's nothing in it. It doesn't mean to say I don't love my wife.'

Roy met his friend's wife thirty years later 'looking hot. Always was a beautiful woman which is why I couldn't understand her husband's infidelity.' She said she had split from her husband the moment her kids were adult. She had known about his infidelities all along but had to consider the children, who now cold-shouldered the father who had become a sad, bald, fat fellow in the corner of the pub.

I don't know what is the female equivalent of sad, bald and fat but it's probably hard, skinny and plastered in make-up. Either way, keep your prejudices in fine working order if you want to stay this side of the moral dividing line. You have to scare yourself into good behaviour.

The question is whether great sex is worth the dispensing of morality. Think of the word 'demoralise'. What does that mean? Demoralisation happens when your morality is removed, as in adultery. A man without morality is demoralised. The first thing somebody does when he does wrong is to excuse, deny and justify what he has done.

Even Saddam Hussein justified his cruel regime by saying: 'When we are cruel to others, we know that our cruelty is in order to bring them back to their true selves.'

The last thing the wrongdoer does is admit he has done wrong. Kim, who ran off with my wife, confided to his sister-in-law that he no longer knew what was right or wrong. He had given up the struggle. He was demoralised.

The two extremes of sexual misbehaviour are prostitutes, performers of porn and swingers on the one hand and Anna Karenina on the other.

Jean Findlay, my sister-in-law, produced and directed a play about strippers called *Call me Susan*. She had to do a lot of research and she said she had never met a prostitute whose spirit was not ruined. She had never even met a stripper who had not been what she called 'hardened' by the experience. She saw them privately after the act was over. It tallies with what Traci Lord, the author of *Underneath It All*, a memoir of her working life as a porn star in the US sex industry, said: 'I've never met a happy porn star.'

I saw a cock doc about an adult movie star on television the other night and from it I learnt that most porn stars are victims of childhood abuse and neglect although the subject of the documentary, Stacey was not.

Stacey said she loved the attention she got from being a porn star. She advised young girls who might want to model themselves on her not to go into the sex industry solely for the money. 'You have got to love sex.'

'I only have sex at work,' she said. 'At home I have my cats.'

'I never get touched out of affection. Like that,' she said, putting a gentle finger on her arm, as if getting her own attention to say something to herself. 'It is always sexual,' she adds with what an air, I thought, of deep regret.

There is a horrible thing called DP. It stands for double penetration and I am afraid it means two men having sex with you, front and back. The documentary eavesdrops on a phone call from an old school friend back home and she says with pride: 'I have just done my first DP!'

At an awards ceremony in Cannes she is approached by a millionaire admirer whom she then agrees to go on a date. Off camera he gave her a lot of money for the inevitable intercourse. She throws the cash all over her bed. She says obviously she would never have had sex with the man without payment. She has no concept of prostitution. No shame. No knowledge. No sense of right and wrong.

An executive from the porn film company says about his per-formers: 'Getting paid a lot of money to screw sexy beautiful people is everybody's idea of heaven. Nothing in the rest of their lives is going to compare with it.'

The only person Stacey cares for is her mother who is very proud of her success as a porn star. There is a scene when mother and daughter dissolve into tears. Her mother wants her to settle down with a man but her latest relationship with a fellow performer has folded after just six weeks. I thought she never brought her work home with her but obviously she had made an exception of this guy.

She has received corrective cosmetic surgery for lips, thighs and boobs making, I assume, everything bigger. 'The idea is to look unreal. We are the objects of fantasy,' she explains.

She takes great professional pride in having won an industry award at Cannes. She comes across as a well-spoken, decent sort of person but she is completely devoid of charm and without a drop of humour. I would say she is graceless.

Adultery is Suspension of Reality

Of course, most female adulterers at the other end of the sexual spectrum see themselves as Anna Karenina without the ending. We don't hurl ourselves under trains. That's so Russian. No, we do the brave face, hence the surfeit of make-up and in extreme cases, dark glasses.

The problem about adultery is how much you lose: either a little or a lot of your reputation, your respectability even in this tolerant age, the respect, not the love, of your children and your own self-regard. And, of course, there's your erstwhile spouse to consider. You will have forfeited his or her good opinion.

And old age can stretch out before you when these are the very things that matter most. So you irretrievably lose them and all for what? Love? Come on. How can you love somebody you have, relatively speaking, only just met? I am jaundiced by personal experience but I think that its infatuation that so often causes adultery. It is just a thing of pleasure and like all things of this world, subject to the Law of Diminishing Returns.

I will tell you what love is. Love is sacrifice. It's what parents effortlessly feel for their children and you should measure all subsequent intimate relationships up against that high ideal. It crucified Anna Karenina.

Supposing your fancy boyfriend or girlfriend was suddenly struck down by an incapacitating stroke, what would you feel then? Methinks he or she would be gently let down after a decent period of sympathy and then allowed to suffer by his or herself – the secrecy of the affair providing perfect cover for the abandonment.

Refused adultery is the basis of all good marriage – not that you don't want it but you simply will not allow yourself to have it because you are not a complete blithering idiot. Who wants to invite Mr. Carnage into his home unless he has got a very good reason? 'My husband has co-habitable defects,' and, 'I am in love with somebody else,' are not good reasons.

Of course . . . of course, there is an exception to every rule, but it is surprising how frequent is the rule and how rare the exception.

In fact, I think adultery is so self-damaging that it is barely rational. Does it happen practically by accident, in which case you wake up one morning having been cuckolded, or maybe it is done by osmosis, so the faithful wife becomes a scarlet woman without anybody quite knowing how? What I am trying to get at is that sometimes actuality removes the connection between one moment and the next. It is as if there is no causal link.

I heard a lovely theory of adultery the other night from some female sceptic. My diary omitted to tell me who. It just says: 'Women try to keep their menfolk happy. Every man in the security of his home inflates himself with the permanent thought: "Here I am. I am the one." And the woman thinks: "Yes. Yes. I hear you. Let's see what I can do to maintain this illusion that I was briefly taken in by in our courtship days. I must somehow now maintain that belief despite mounting evidence to the contrary.'"

Of course when the illusion goes, the marriage needs to get real or people may start having affairs to create other fabulous illusions – somebody else the wife can believe in or some other impressionable woman who can believe in the husband.

The problem is that however it is accomplished, once adultery has begun, the craziness starts and before you know where you are, people start burbling on about fate and even worse, soul mates.

Before embarking on a course of action that involves adultery, I really recommend reading Howard Jacobson's *Who's Sorry Now?* He pretty comprehensively covers the subject, giving all the advantages and disadvantages, and he sweetens the pill of instruction with a narrative of high entertainment value.

Hedonism does not satisfy, as even Hitler realised. George Orwell attributed Hitler's rise to power to this one fact. He wrote: 'Hitler grasped the falsity of the hedonistic attitude to life.' Hitler realised people had a crying need to believe in something bigger than physical satisfaction and he gave them the doctrine of National Socialism.

Drugs are Very Depressing

The world also offers a cocktail of drink and drugs, pretty good fun in the short term and even a plausible lifestyle choice within moderation, although I think few people will dispute that drugs are a young man's game.

I heard a wonderful true story about coke from my sister-in-law JJ that celebrates British sangfroid even in the midst of a drugs orgy. We all know what coke does in general. It's a very selfish drug. No one listens although you think you are brilliant. It gives you the illusion of ultimate truths being made known to you. And you feel ashamed the next day of having revealed intimacies to party acquaintances although if the other person is on coke the chances are they will not have remembered your embarrassing confidences. Coke is a social cop out because it guarantees you a good time without any effort on your part. It lowers boundaries and so can lead to arbitrary sex, which observation leads seamlessly to JJ's story.

When she was in her early twenties she found herself at a trendy dinner party in somebody's flat. Everyone had come in couples. It was a vodka and coke party and then dinner – only the coke was the drug not the fizzy drink. The sit down dinner got under way in a civilised fashion with conversation flowing rapidly. Towards the end of dinner JJ went to the toilet to have a pee. The door was unlocked so she went in and was shocked and astonished to find two of the young women, mostly naked, locked in a lesbian embrace. They looked up from what I might call their heavy petting and invited her to join in and JJ said that was very kind but she wanted a pee.

'And did you?'

'Well, yes. There was only the one loo in the house and I couldn't wait. I didn't know how long they were going to go on for and I felt it was rather intrusive of me to ask them to hurry up because I was desperate for a pee.'

To be utterly honest, I only wrote that drugs were a young man's game to look cool and also to set the tone of nonchalant worldliness for the JJ story. In actual fact I think it is a mug's game and I think the reason that anti-depressant prescriptions have quadrupled in this country in the last twenty years is, so has drug-taking. Actually, it has gone through the roof since my day. At least when I was young, taking hard drugs was a definite moral decision, like having an abortion. Now it is the cultural norm for youth.

The government should mount a poster campaign with the slogan: 'Taking drugs in your youth means having to take drugs in your middle-age: Anti-depressants.'

Drugs obviously play havoc with your serotonins and endorphins to create these artificial chemically induced feelings of euphoria and the inevitable mental compensation that has to take place to restate the balance of your mind is depression. It is just like our artificial credit boom over the last quarter of a century. The financial drug of choice was the derivative and now all that consumption is producing serious, long lasting financial depression. There is always pay back-time.

Drink Reduces a Problem to Soluble Matter

Now my attitude to drink is very different. As you can see from the title of this book, it is one of my best friends but it is a moody bugger and by that I mean it plays around with your moods – not unlike its big brother, drugs. Abigail Thaw said of her alcoholic father, the TV actor John Thaw, that as a child she only understood his behaviour in the house when she started to put things together. 'Ah so the drink in his hand means he'll be grumpy in a couple of hours.' (*Sunday Times*, 14 April 2013)

Alcohol has got a lot to say for itself. In fact half the time you can't get it to shut up. It certainly opens up Highlanders who are proverbially two nips short of humanity. Supposedly put a couple of whiskies into an Invernessian and he will overcome his natural shyness and start to entertain the idea of a conversation. Furthermore, alcohol takes you in either of two ways or a mixture of both. It makes you into a truth teller or playful – both tremendously positive things. So alcohol can be a force for the good.

I think the prize for the most profound thing ever said about alcohol comes from Homer Simpson, with Freud and T. S. Eliot coming up close on the inside rail. Homer Simpson famously said: 'Drink is the solution and also the problem.' Apart from the wisdom of that remark, I also love the pun on the word: 'solution'.

Part of the allure of alcohol is seeing it in its beautifully labelled bottle. Then there is the ritual of the unscrewing or uncorking or the decapitation of a lid and the *phut* of compressed air being released. Maybe your drink calls for the *clunk click* of a couple of ice cubes. Maybe it even needs some fruit and veg, as in the case of a fancy cocktail. And Oh look, you are standing back to let fly a champagne cork at the ceiling. Now you are pouring and there is a different sound and you have got to get the right glass for the right drink. Now the glass is filling up with colour and this drink is producing a satisfactory creamy white foam and that one is fizzing with sparkling bubbles and this entire cabaret show has happened even before you have taken a sip. It is not boring like drugs, where you just pop a pill in your mouth or worse still, act as if you are going to the doctors.

As with everything there is a right way and a wrong way of doing drink and I know I do it wrongly so I have to be careful. Remember in *Brideshead Revisited* when the Italian mistress of the banished Earl says that Sebastian was an alcoholic not because of how much he drank but why he drank. That line jumped out at me. I am not one of these people who have a couple of drinks to relax at the end of a stressful day or like a civilised woman who fancies taking a glass of wine with her meal. I drink to get transported into a heightened frame of mind, an altered state of being. The absolute minimum I can drink at one sitting is a pint of beer and a bottle of wine.

I drink at parties because it obliterates the racket of other people's conversations and it helps me concentrate on the one I am having. Also, I drink because it bridges gaps. It can have a humanising effect. Also, it is very difficult to make friends with other men without drink. Sometimes I drink and think: 'O hello this is who I really am!' Or to put it another way, I think I drink for existential reasons. 'I drink therefore I am'.

Not as silly as it sounds. Freud, who did not believe in God, replaced Him with drink, jokes and art. He said these were the only three possible viable reactions to the frustrations of life. So you see, alcohol is not just a liquid refreshment, it is a fantastically important element made available for man by which he can live and have his being.

'Man cannot bear too much reality,' was T. S. Eliot's famous dictum and alcohol gives you sufficient illusion to make the whole business of life tolerable. I had to give up alcohol for a while because I found myself allergic to it and then after a couple of weeks I experimented with the hay fever allergy pill, Claritin, and thank God it worked for me but in the hellish two week interval, I wrote this in my diary:

> Due to my allergy I have had to cut alcohol out of my life and it is incredible what a fundamental change it makes to your general outlook. I now realise I used to associate life with alcohol. In other words I would rush through my daily encounters to get on with the next thing to be done or else just seek out the conversational highs and not bother with proper personal connection. I only really engaged with people through alcohol. And even so, my alcoholic social life was just a roundabout way of me taking pleasure in myself through other people.
>
> Now I have got nothing to look forward to. There is no automatic pleasure. I have got to earn it all myself. And there is no difference between day and night. Now I have to take pleasure in other people in conversation.

Alcoholism forced a fellow called Rikki, who is a friend of a friend, to go teetotal and he said: 'it makes the dull bits of life better and the fun bits not as good.' Elizabeth Taylor famously found Richard Burton a bore without drink. No wonder he developed a drink problem. I am incredibly ambivalent about drink. I can't work out whether it is good or bad for me.

CHAPTER FIVE

The Crowd is Mightier
than the Word

A common mistake of youth is to overestimate your own personal independence and pooh-pooh the power of the group; under twenty-five, you can feel so superior to the world about you, up to its neck in compromise. Youth has the luxury of being able to look down on the people who have gone before them.

Over twenty-five, in the world of work, and you very quickly find yourself having to do stuff at other people's behest and it often flies in the face of what you believe in. It leaves you open to accusations of hypocrisy. People stop reading serious fiction because it reflects badly on them. They dismiss debate about the meaning of life and any form of idealism as 'heavy' and essentially boring and they put as much distance as possible between themselves and their previous incarnation as adolescents themselves. Out of the mouths of stand-up comedians come fully articulated, perfected barbs of fury against the system sublimated into humour. It is all they can do now to nourish their souls because books take too long to read, churches are to be avoided and no one believes in politics any more.

But in the good old days how we enjoyed the total contempt of young revolutionaries for the establishment. We were all young then, especially the rank and file, who were going to man the barricades and occasionally dodge bullets in the East or go on protest marches and battle bad weather in the West. Of course, youth has achieved great things like the defeat of Communism in Eastern Europe and the launch of the hippy movement in the Western world, but too often you can feel that here are these skinny little whippersnappers with a lot of feeling and very few facts, ranting away about what is wrong with the status quo and even when they are right in their criticism, they can fail to realise that very often it is the least bad option given the circumstances. History provides us with many graphic examples of the cure being worse than the disease.

And what is true of government can be doubly true of how people conduct themselves in their private lives because people tend to behave a lot better in public than in private. How many young offspring look at their broken down, cowed and complicated parents with all the many obvious things that are wrong with them and make a solemn private resolution not to end up like that? They may well carry out a perceptive analysis of their parents' particular forms of neurosis and fail to realise their own different methods of cocking up their lives, which will only become truly apparent when they themselves set up home and create their own mad two-man cultures, if I might be so bold as to use that expression to describe marriage.

There is nothing a teenager likes better than to feel outrage at middle-age compliance because it makes him feel superior and it is the work of a moment to turn that disdain into satire, the comedy of choice for youth. That is, of course, why so many first rate television satirists have been young guys fresh out of university, bristling with pristine integrity, untouched by engagement with the world. They could give their comedy the full cutting edge of their scorn.

It is not as if these brilliant comedians are any better at living than the rest of us. In fact, if you delve into their private lives you discover that their level of carnage is generally worse than the average. You can put that down to the pressures of creative work, the inducements of fame, the tears of the clown or the inevitable separation between word and deed where actuality finds the gaps. Certainly Jimmy Carr's personal tax arrangements found a sizeable hole in his much prized integrity that allowed him to expose public figures to ridicule on a weekly basis – greed being a familiar theme of his. That is the final thing to bear in mind. Taking the piss out of something is easy compared to actually getting out there and doing it yourself.

It was the optimism and ignorance of youth that made me brave enough to strike out on my own culturally and financially. My arrogance empowered me to break free of the restrictions of the group. I dismissed as second rate people who I felt had become intellectually ossified. I felt most people abdicated life. They just wanted to tick along doing the normal things. What ambition they had was financial. What about the all-important journey to the centre of your being? What about breaking down class barriers? What about attempting the good life? What about self-expression? What about real connection? What about social conscience? What about personal growth?

Live intelligence I took to mean the ability to grow, in other words, change. I kept my mind in mint condition by reading only the best of literature and maintaining my red diary, mockingly code-named by my wife as *The Thoughts of Chairman Chief.* My child-hood nickname amongst the cousins had been 'Chiefy'. Sarah used to see me lost in thought and describe me with a roll of her eyes 'as nibbling my knuckles and thinking my big thoughts'.

I eschewed the safer paths of employment provided by the system and started off as an independent entrepreneur. Free accommodation was a definite help, courtesy of my parents, and my timing was lucky in that credit was comparatively cheap and easily available and the property market was vertical. None of my businesses made money as such but they stayed this side of liquidation. They also actually paid my living expenses and here's the clincher: I would house them in property which would double in value every five years. There was my profit, which I would roll over into the next business in bigger premises, having syphoned off some of the capital gains to pay for an enhanced lifestyle.

But the smugness stops there because as the years rolled by I began to realise what I was badly losing out on. My independence came at a terrible cost. I was inspired by writers and thinkers like John O'Donohue who wrote dismissively about people who sacrificed their own individuality to adhere to the mentality of the group: 'With the hammer of second-hand thoughts they beat this rich internal landscape into a mono-scape. They make themselves conform. They agree to fit in. They cease to be vivid presences, even to themselves.'

Passages like that would make me hug myself with self-gratification. I was on the right path. I was ploughing the lonely furrow of the true artist. There were only two snags though that emerged in the course of my middle-age. Other people, who were not so precious about their internal landscape, made a priority of simply getting on with other people. Vivid presence be damned, what concerned them in their social lives was the Holy Grail of Popularity! That was their choice, not mine. We would see who came out on top.

The primary snag I found was that as the years went by I noticed that my friends and neighbours in our social group were actually developing in a more rounded way than myself. They certainly appeared to be gaining handsomely in self-confidence. They should be getting richer than me, not more mature. Dammit! The theory seemed to be backfiring.

The reason was this. The group normally beats the individual because its members have one another, which means building up over the years a wealth of mutual reference and a common lexicon of shared language, whereas the rebel, or free thinker, as he might describe himself, is out on his own with no one really to talk to. Nevertheless, he has actually to take part in the group because you cannot cut yourself entirely. The disadvantage is that, as he does not subscribe to its ideology, he gradually loses a certain fluency of expression. Everybody else, on the other hand, speaks with conviction because they have long since forgotten that they don't believe what they say. Oh yes, and the other snag? Talent . . .

If you want to know how flimsy is the individual operating outside the orbit of the group, you need look no further than a rueful comment from Sebastian, a character created by Vita Sackville West in her book *The Edwardians* about marriage between people of different classes: 'We could never hit it off for long. There was never anything but love to keep us together.'

Choose your social circle with care because they are your world and it normally means a dozen people. There is an argument for ruthlessness but for most people it is too much effort and they put up with the most convenient people for the rest of their lives, and that very often means family. Obviously the solution is to surround yourself with like-minded people but that was not so easy in the country where I lived. Maybe that is one of the restrictions of life in the provinces but still you have the huge consolation of nature.

Anyway, money tends to rule the roost in the city and that too has the effect of dispersing one's kindred spirits. The Richard Curtis films and a lot of American sitcoms like *Friends* buy into that particular fantasy. The core group is half a dozen cool, good looking people between the ages of twenty-five and thirty-five. Throw in a wheelchair here or a black man there for the sake of political correctness, it is still pure elitism. It is in the nature of a social group, even if it is made up of people cherry-picked from tried and tested friends, to become self-enclosed and that brings its own issues like narrow-mindedness and complacency.

There is a far better solution and it only took me a couple of decades to stumble across it. Dualism is the answer. You have got to live a double life. Treat the discourse of the group as a very important foreign language you have to master for the sake of social ease. And there is nothing to stop you putting your own spin on it. Then couched in the pages of your diary, you can develop your own interior monologue, just like prayer, which should be an intimate, life-long conversation with the Lord. No one else needs to hear it. Reading feeds this secret life.

You end up like an iceberg with only your top ten per cent showing as you glide into old age, the submerged element taking a greater and greater part of your consciousness, as you spend longer by yourself with less and less to distract the surface of your mind. It will be your diaries that will now stand you in good stead. Old age is the time where your secret life will really be coming into its own. You have been training for this stage your entire thinking life.

The top tenth of the iceberg is important for social interaction but old age is where the other nine tenths help you enjoy this period of silent contemplation, reviewing your own life and watching other people's and preparing yourself for the final adventure – departure from this world into the next (and we all know there will be several dummy runs at death). Each one will involve discomfort if not pain and days, weeks and maybe months alone in bed.

By the end of your life you want to feel that you belong to a country, a town, a neighbourhood, to a family, a place of work, a hobby group, a social set, and maybe even a church or a football club. You become inconspicuous.

The whole point of going away is so that you can come back. Joseph Campbell in *The Hero's Journey* says that challenges come your way in life and you should recognise them and then grasp them with all your might. These great opportunities only come two or three times in your life which is why it is so important not to balk at them. Of course, these crises will take you out of your comfort zone away from your peer group, and there will be a time when you have to battle against the odds all by yourself. The experience will teach you a lot about life and be the making of you. But then there comes the time when you are ready for the return journey back home. That is old age, the final lap of honour.

Looking back on it, I think I seized my three moments which were university, the pit and marriage although I appear to have failed all three challenges. I failed to fully engage my workmates down the pit but I nevertheless totally broke down my sense of social superiority bequeathed at birth, nourished at public school, confirmed at university and for most other people of my ilk, sustained in a professional career. To this day I take no service for granted. I never, for example, go to the supermarket checkout without speculating about the life, looks and character of the person serving me and I am quietly envious of the tough guys on the building site. I am genuinely egalitarian, which is not as common as you might imagine in class-bound Britain. I am, for example, currently in love with a waitress.

Going to university at the age of twenty-six was a risk but well worth it. No one can call a 2/2 sign of a successful career at university and it reflected a dilettante attitude to my studies but nevertheless reading and conversation in my leisure time did genuinely awaken in me a life-long intellectual curiosity. University did what it should do. It not only gave me the language of analysis but it also taught me to question everything. However, my real regret is that it did not lead to a professional career which would have given me an expertise.

Obviously, marriage is the boldest move we make. It is an amazing decision and I love it for its hope, value and total lack of cynicism. It is also deeply calculating. I took full advantage of my seniority as a mature student and married the most beautiful girl on the campus with a PhD brain. Obviously, I had married beyond myself and there would come a time in her development when she would go whizzing past me. I never knew it was going to last as long as twenty-five years. We were hugely ambitious and attempted a 'D. H. Lawrentian' union, you know: mind, body, soul and I found it profoundly satisfying. Obviously, I cannot speak for Sarah but she appeared to be enjoying it too.

Amazingly, the break-up of the marriage, which put me in trauma for a couple of years, eventually turned out to have a hugely liberating effect on me. It freed me from the growing oppression of her superiority and it cracked me wide open to receive the attentions of other people. My marriage had been a bolt hole and allowed me not to take seriously the social life that took place all around me. On the other hand, separation and divorce threw me back on my own resources and made me feel independent. It allowed me to rebalance myself.

Failure is the great teacher in the sky. Success is merely an ego pump.

Horses Race Home

I think when you wed, what you have learnt from your outward journey into the big bad world to what you have inherited from where you come from, a tremendous integrity takes place, a feeling of wholesomeness. Later in life you reconsider your background and you appreciate it anew and this time you can see so much more about why your parents behaved the way they did and how you are not so different to them after all. In his last years D. H. Lawrence famously reassessed his father, a coalminer married to a school teacher. Previously he had dismissed him as an ignorant, oppressive brute. It was only in his later years he came to appreciate him for his virility and other qualities not to be found in the sophisticated drawing rooms of Bloomsbury.

It is only later in life that you appreciate the less obvious, what I call the quieter virtues, like dignity, stoicism, patience, tolerance, consideration, good manners, empathy, tact, diplomacy, supportiveness, engagement. These virtues are not as glamorous as wit, intelligence, eloquence, imagination and beauty and you need time to notice them. They are the sort of things that are picked up by servants and employees and other second-class citizens, like the old. My grandmother used to accuse my beautiful sister, Sophia, of being selfish because she was slow in offering to help over the domestic chores. Members of her peer group did not mind a jot. Any old fool could do the washing up. You try and keep four guys happy at a party at the same time without any of them getting jealous. Now that is a rare skill. She grew a heart in later life and now it is her turn to belabour her own daughters.

Now you can look at your own background and see from an outsider's perspective. I have always been terribly critical of my own background but there is a lot to admire in the sheer style and chutzpah of people who successfully epitomise their culture. All you have to do is let go your high-minded prejudices to enjoy the spectacle. You should take your lead from your grandchildren who are so quick to laugh at any idiosyncrasies of their grandparents, happy to indulge them in their old fashioned opinions. It is a marvellous release not to take people seriously. Another privilege of old age in our culture is that you are so unimportant that no one is scared of you. This allows you to talk to people of other generations as equals and let them have a good laugh, affectionately perhaps, but nevertheless, at your expense.

My mother has never told a joke in her life. She has never even tried to be funny any more than her exact contemporary, Maggie Thatcher, who once famously announced that every woman 'needed a willy'. I think she was actually referring to her deputy, Willie Whitelaw. Similarly, my mother once announced to a table full of adolescent grandchildren that she loved to come down to a good cox in the morning. She had married an apple farmer and was fondly reminiscing. The grandchildren were in bits.

On another occasion she put her nephew-in-law, the bombastic and celebrated travel writer and historian, William Dalrymple, in his place when she said: 'I don't know why you make such a fuss about literature. All you need to write a book is good eyesight.' She based this last observation on her experience of writing her privately published: *The War Memorials of The Highlands and Other Significant Monuments* which primarily involved her copying inscriptions off gravestones.

An old person should be like a novelist, an amused and knowing spectator fascinated by all the permutations of behaviour and drunk with love of dialogue, as interested in the surface of interaction as in the meaning of what has been transacted before her or his very eyes. Jane Austen is our model. She took an active part in the social whirl that went on about her, privately hoarding all the intricacies of behaviour in a notebook or even on a chance piece of paper, which she would slip under a newspaper or behind a book if anyone noticed her. Old age should make fifth columnists of the lot of us. We have got to entertain ourselves somehow. I squirrelled away just a simple little house visit the other night and then quickly bunged it into my diary to enjoy at leisure. I will share it with you to show what I mean:

A marriage creates a culture of two behind closed doors, where lots of little peccadilloes of manner and speech, which reflect the merging of two personalities attracted, then bonded to one another in a relationship intended forever. I visited the newly married Jura and Rachel and with them the process had already started. There was a pile of copper coins heaped on the kitchen table showing their extreme frugality, as if it was normal to save pennies in this world of pound coins and plastic money. There was a bottle of Desaranno on the shelf, the only alcohol in the house, and I drew attention to it. Rachel said: 'Yes, we have it with our cocoa.' I can just imagine Jura shouting through to the kitchen. 'Knock me up a cocoa will you, Rachel, and make it a double.' Previously I had been shown round their mutual workshop – one end for Jura's carpentry and the other for Rachel's pottery. 'How often do you pot?' 'Oh, four or five times' a week.' 'What, an hour a time?' 'Good God, no, I get lost in it. Sometimes I am here for four or five hours throwing pots.' Such a funny phrase: 'I am just going next door Jura, to throw some pots,' as if they have just had an argument and she needed to trash some crockery.

Belonging

When you are cast out on your own, as old people inevitably are, the one thing you crave is belonging. A group provides that cover. It is not the prominence you have spent your life striving for that sets you up above your fellow man that defeats the solitude of old age, but community. You just want to be part of a bigger thing than yourself.

'Within a group everyone has a place including the creep, third from the back,' says my daughter, Angie, who has noticed how her workforce at Hootananny has successfully bonded under her benevolent management. 'Without the creep, everybody else would not be feeling quite so good about themselves.' An old person can be that creep.

Creep, I say, creep into a group and when you are gone, they will think something is missing. You then reappear and everybody, without quite knowing why, feels better again. We might be inconspicuous but we can make ourselves felt. Meantime, you feel something as well: that all important sense of belonging.

'Everybody's fine once you get used to them,' says Angie. 'You even get to like them if you see them often enough and even if they turn out to be absolutely impossible, you get a hell of a laugh when they are gone.' Highly idiosyncratic people can be accommodated in a group, be remembered with fondness and forgiven their peccadillos, and let's face it, age can make people pretty cranky. It all depends on their spirit. A group with a good spirit – like a happy family or a well-run office where staff are treated like people rather than organic work units – is home.

I created a restaurant: The Joy of Taste, based on that very principle. The idea was that everybody should offer their services free of charge for one shift a week in return for a meal and a glass of wine at the end of the shift or a voucher that would entitle them to a free meal at any time of their choosing, apart from Saturdays, which were expected to be full and so that would mean them displacing an actual paying customer. The Joy of Taste was being proposed as a friendship club with benefits and, as you might expect, I was assured by all and sundry that it could not possibly work.

'Who on earth is going to work for nothing?'

'They are not working for nothing. I am offering friendship on a plate.'

'Do you really think anybody is going to fall for that?'

'One person per shift means I will have a waiting staff of twenty. That is a lot of friends. The national average is three. And I will tell you something else: the hustle and bustle of a busy restaurant is more fun than four bare walls with only the television for company. You don't have to watch *EastEnders* and *Coronation Street*, you can actually be in The Joy of Taste. They are just three communities but only one of them is real. All I know is that you work hard for four hours, waiting at table in a busy restaurant and you have bonded with your fellow waiters. I don't know a faster, more effective way of making a friend. It is better than a hundred cocktail parties. All I know is that loneliness is a national scandal. Something needs to be done about it and this is something.'

'What you don't know is how to run a restaurant especially when it's not really busy,' was one critic's telling reply.

Those last words turned out to be prophetic because although the comparatively old, the infirm, the lame and the lonely came hobbling through the door offering their services as free waiters and waitresses, they were not immediately followed by customers in sufficient numbers to make the restaurant viable and over the ensuing two and a half years, I lost £250,000 without really noticing it. I don't mean that I had so much money that £250,000 was just a financial blip. In actual fact it was all my money. It is just that I had such fun with my staff who for the first time ever were actually my age and I had such fun trying to a make a go of the restaurant which soon came to look busy enough that I did not notice the money quietly haemorrhaging out of the business. That is the scary thing about business. Because of a 30-day credit offered by suppliers, losses can accrue silently without you being alerted. You have got to be half full on a cold November Tuesday – that is the test of success in the restaurant business – not high on adrenaline and drunk on free wine after a packed summer Saturday night with a lot of lovely, late middle-aged freedom fighters on day release from the prison of their front living rooms!

I am glad to report that it looks as if the restaurant is now finally breaking even but, more interestingly, the social theory has worked a treat and friendships have broken out all over the place. We have probably had fifty people through our books since we started. Some people stay for a few months, half a dozen of us have been there from the very beginning. An NOP survey published in May 1993 reported that only 4 per cent of Britons were happy in their work. Well, we are definitely part of that minority because we have put people before pounds. We have created a little community for ourselves.

When you are cast out on your own, as old people inevitably are, the one thing you crave is belonging. A group provides that cover. This is why.

CHAPTER SIX

Looking Back in Candour

There are two contradictory impulses in man to belong and to excel, to be part of the group and to be individual. Children just want to be gang members. Teenage fantasy is all about becoming a rock star. Middle-aged people are forced to conform by circumstances. The old man is expelled from the community by dint of retirement. He is out on his own. Age has sidelined him.

I agree with the Ancient Greeks who believed that you should always seek the Golden Mean. They were right about most things and they are right about this. The key to life is balance, which means you should encourage self-expression in your children, crush the egotism of youth like the way the army does to its recruits, and middle-aged people should at all costs keep alight within themselves wild dreams of freedom and self-expression. I, personally, on the brink of old age, am going to devote my last quadrant to returning to the fold. Odysseus has been on his odyssey; now Homer is coming home.

I will give you my potted history. I will offer myself up as a case study. That way I don't offend anybody. I will serve myself up on a platter for your delectation.

'That's enough now. Get on with it,' as my brother, Rory would say to me.

First a prelude: Every life tells a story and by old age you ought to know what's your particular one. The structure of the narrative will follow the same pattern. A life is not a short story, unless you have the misfortune to die in childhood. Every book is the same. If you don't believe me, try out this model of analysis on the novel you are currently reading. Every book has forces of oppression and a freedom fighter.

A naughty little narrative trick that never fails to work on the reader is to get him or her to sympathise and identify with the hero. Give him a particular hard time at the hands of his oppressor in the first fifty pages, creating feelings of outrage in the sucker – I mean Dear Reader. In real life that corresponds to a bad childhood which any half decent psychotherapist can persuade you that you have had. Neglect is good but abuse is better. As a rule of thumb, divorce does the business. Unfortunately, my parents had a particularly happy marriage, but I was saved by having been barbarously banished from home and sent away to boarding school at such an early age, any professional counsellor would testify it qualified as abandonment, a particularly fine form of neglect.

But to return to my model of literary criticism, I have noticed with literature that there is always a book-long struggle which the hero wins against impossible odds and usually gets the girl. The girl is an optional extra but we do like him to get her. Change the sexes according to whether you are reading Jane Austen or Jeffrey Archer.

The eventual triumph of the chief protagonist might appear to be a failure to the outside world but we, the readers, are educated by the author that, according to his terms, it is in reality a victory. Every writer has his or her message. Every book has its theme. Your tub is being thumped. In the course of the book the hero will, at least, have gained in understanding and, by transference, so will have the reader.

The author is God and he creates the world in which his characters come into conflict. Actually half the time, especially in contemporary books where modern man spends his life trying to find himself, the person the hero is locked in mortal combat with is, of course, himself. Look at both Amises, D. H. Lawrence, Virginia Woolf, E. M. Forster, Graham Greene and the American triumvirate: Philip Roth, John Updike and Saul Bellow – in fact, quite frankly, most of the biggies in this self-obsessed secular age. 'Her rival, the enemy whom she hoped to dispossess and drive into exile, if not extinction, was her own constrained and terrified self,' writes Philip Roth about his hero's second wife, Susan in *My Life as a Man*. We used to obsess about God. Now we obsess about ourselves. I suppose shooting yourself is better than shooting other people. So that is progress.

What is your story? What is your battle? First, you have got to look deep inside and ask yourself the two most searching questions in life. What are your fears? What are your desires? Life is just a negotiation between these two primal impulses.

I only had three fears: workers, women and intellectuals. I only had three desires: goodness, truth and beauty. Like most people, I started out in life determined to be a good person and I have not wavered from that point of view in the last half century.

Truth is Habit, Gandalf

Sending me away to boarding school put me off lying, not that I was ever that keen on it. My mother adopted a brilliant policy of not smacking us four boys no matter what we had done, as long as we told the truth. It got you into the habit but what really clinched it for me was my private education – nothing but lies! The very name was a lie. It was not a public school. Members of the public were precisely the people who could not go to it. You had to belong to the moneyed elite.

The lies and betrayals start on your very first day at school. Throughout the holidays leading up to this moment, your parents have been very upbeat about the prospect but now suddenly your mother won't get out of the car. The sun is shining but she's got the windscreen wiper on at full speed. She's crying so much she thinks it's raining. The betrayals come in thick and fast now. Your older brother has left your side and joined his pals and he won't recognise you now until the return journey home at the end of term. Your father has let go of your tiny hand. He thinks it's unmanly. And he too has become a liar. 'It'll soon be holidays.'

It's a new regime with crazy rules. You get beaten for the crime of talking after lights out. At home the very best conversations between me and my brother, Anselm, in our shared a bedroom, happened after lights-out.

At Moreton Hall it seemed that half our teachers, whom we had to look up to as pillars of respectability and models of behaviour, were pedophiles. One fellow gave us a Mars bar each if we ran around naked in the woods. Well, the clothes were off our backs in no time. He was as good as his word. We got a whole one each. At home if we ever got a Mars bar, we always had to halve it with a brother.

But what really bugged me was that no matter how hard I worked at my studies, I was never allowed to beat my older brother, Rory. Because of where our birthdays fell in the calendar and, to cut a long story short, I was bright and Rory was thick – we were put in the same class. The teachers were not allowed to place me above Rory in form order in case he developed an inferiority complex. Rory cottoned on to this and cruised through his exams on the back of my swottishness. I wonder how thick he really was.

Human consideration was allowed to override the fruits of endeavour. It was like rigging election results. It told me even recognition could be a lie. It was also certainly an early lesson of how success is not necessarily a question of what you know; because I knew the pluperfect subjunctive of the verb 'to love' backwards in Latin, Greek, French and English, while Rory had that faraway look of somebody who was on a prison diet, dreaming of home cooking. Yes, it is true that if you have been to an old-fashioned prep school, prison is not such a shock to the system, which is why all those scandalous MPs sail through the experience.

Beauty is Outrageous

Beauty has been my abiding problem, especially when it is attached to a woman. I have been seriously distracted by it throughout my life. I don't know if I am like most men but I suffer from a bad case of Wandering Eye Disease. I have never got onto any form of public transport without first scanning all the women aboard for beauty and/or sex appeal. I have never walked down a street and allowed a beautiful woman to walk past me without noticing her. I can clock quite a sizeable crowd and spot the lookers. And this visual illness has not diminished with age.

All I can say with all my heart is that I desire beauty. It is unfair. It is outrageous. These women do not deserve my slavish devotion. They have not done anything special except materialise in front of me. Everybody has got a weakness and that is mine. Obviously I have got others as well but they are merely inadequacies.

My love of beauty could get me into trouble. I prefer, for example, Jill to God. Jill is the woman with whom I am currently enamoured, but she is married. She certainly wipes the floor with God in terms of her command of my imagination and her grip on my heart and obviously, as regards my genitalia, you will not be surprised to hear that there is no contest. Temptation is only not an issue because, thankfully, she does not return my feelings. Sarah preferred Kim to God. I do understand and I don't want to be put to the test. That is why I pray every day: 'And lead us not into temptation.'

Supposing Jill suddenly, by some miracle, made herself available to me. The only thing that would prevent me from succumbing to her charms would be fear. I mean fear is a good thing in certain circumstances because it can prevent you from causing other people misery. Fear of the Lord is good and yes, I am frightened of Him. You don't want to get in His bad books and He has got a thing about adultery. He doesn't like it at all.

Shyness Beats Sexiness

You never know when temptation will strike. You can put up defences against one person and be ambushed by another where you least expect it, and there is no saying you will not fall by the wayside. Once a year my wife and the children used to go for a week's holiday staying with the in-laws and I was left alone in the house with a long list of instructions. This particular year I had the added responsibility of looking after my little daughter's hamster. Here's the note she left me: 'Give Mango an outing every day. Check his food and water and clean his tray, if necessary. Forget the hamster and you are dead.'

Well, they were no sooner out the door than the bloody thing escaped. I mean you don't want to know the details but obviously the little pest had been working on an escape plan for weeks. Unbeknownst to us, it had secreted a file about its person and had been sawing away at one of the bars of the grill night after night and I imagine it used its little pink hands just to snap that last thread of metal for it to squeeze through and make its dash for freedom.

Obviously, I contacted Air Sea Rescue, Missing Persons Bureau and we had Interpol check all the ports for anybody trying to get out of the country without proper documentation and the Home Secretary had to answer questions on the floor of the House about the parlous state of prison security.

That was the drama that was occupying my mind when a young woman turned up at my door to do an interview for a business studies university post graduate thesis. She needed a typical small independent businessman and I fitted the bill. As a matter of fact, in the course of the interview, we discovered that my practical experience of business perfectly dovetailed her theoretical knowledge and that generally we enjoyed one another's company. The conversation flowed effortlessly and there were plenty of laughs. She was a nice woman and it was getting late so I asked her to join me in a supper which I had already planned to have with some other friends.

At the end of the evening, there was a discussion about where she was to stay the night. Should she book into a local hotel? And I thought: 'This is ridiculous. We're adults. Why shouldn't she stay the night alone in my house just because she happens to be a member of the opposite sex?'

Of course, my pal and fellow diner, Mike, couldn't stop winking at me and nudging me as I escorted him to the car. As for the woman, we went our separate ways to bed. No bother. No issue. What's the problem?

Then in the middle of the night I was woken by the sound of screaming. I rushed through to the spare room and there was this woman standing on her bed screaming at a little hamster that she had seen crawling across her duvet. When I walked in she had grabbed a pillow to cover herself but, as you can imagine, it was insufficient for the task and I could not help but notice that she was well proportioned and also stark naked behind the pillow.

It was only later when I had returned to my bed that my long night of torture began as the immediate sensual memory of the incredible proximity of this nearly naked woman started to play havoc with my genitalia.

Now isn't that funny? It is not the actual event that is sexy, perhaps because it was over so quick. It is the eternal rehashing of the event in your mind's eye that makes you sick with desire. I lay in my bed tossing and turning. Let me rephrase that. Sleep eluded me. My penis was whimpering and I thought, 'Not that hamster again'.

All night long it was a three-cornered fight in my mind between desire, morality and . . . and . . . shyness. Yes shyness, of course. It is not the easiest thing in the world to go into somebody's bedroom with whom you are only on social terms and say something like: 'I would like to apologise on behalf of my hamster but, look, here is a far friendlier animal you might prefer. He's called Roger.' I tell you this, it was the longest night of my life and all I can say is shyness pipped it at the post.

Where there's Fear there's a Way

You make critical decisions extremely early on in life. I was probably aged ten when I consecrated myself to the truth. I was given faith in God by my parents, which was my good fortune, but my decision not to throw it away probably happened at puberty. The other big decision I made was that I preferred to tackle my fundamental fears than remain a boring piece of nothingness, because as a boy you feel like a blank piece of paper – or, at least, that is how I felt about myself.

What I was frightened of then was rugby, which is why I have consciously used the word 'tackle' when dealing with the word 'fear'. I do not think you can divorce the physical from the abstract. I think they are profoundly bound up with one another, which is why bravery in action is proof of moral courage. The greatest test of guts at school, I felt, was tackling on the rugby pitch.

Now, obviously, I hated rugby and always have done. I can't see what there is to like. It is deeply uncomfortable. The weather was invariably appalling and pain was never far away, but at prep school you had to do it, in the winter months, five afternoons a week and six if you were fool enough to be picked for the school team and so had to turn out on Saturdays. Thankfully, I was never strong enough or fast enough to draw the attention of the coach but there was something in me that refused to duck out of a tackle because that had nothing to do with speed, strength or skill. It just required guts and I could not bear to think of myself, or be thought of, as a coward.

If you threw yourself at somebody's bony knees moving like pistons, no matter how big or ferocious the fellow above those knees – and remember size is relative and people had horrible things called growth spurts at prep school – he would fall like a tree cut down by an electric saw. You just had to put your face right against his fractious legs, get your arms round them, hold on tight and down he would come.

My valour on the rugby pitch put me in the right frame of mind when I had to deal with my three big lifetime fears. I was determined to tackle them. It was fear of the unknown that made my youth such a barren time in my dealings with the opposite sex. Up until the day I left school I had lived a life of sexual apartheid. I was brought up with three brothers and was sent to a single sex boarding school. So I did not know anything about the little skirted critters.

Sex is Always Next Door

My theory at the time was that a girl was very like a roe deer. The slightest wrong movement could startle her and she would gracefully bound off out of reach in the opposite direction to you. My adolescent strategy at parties was to single out a girl, spy her from a distance, stalk her, then properly pepped up with nips from the hip flask, you finally jumped on her when she least expected it under the cover of semi-darkness in the twilight hours.

As you can imagine, this tactic did not lead to any lasting relationships. OK, I exaggerate for comic effect, but you get the idea. I will tell you something that isn't funny though and is literally true. I had to wait until the age of twenty-six to lose my virginity. That must be the second saddest line in literature (that is, if you can honour this humble tome with that glorious description). The saddest is: 'Who's turn is it to have Dad for Christmas?' My adult life seems to be sandwiched by grief.

I don't think I can leave the subject of what I can only, unfortunately, call my youthful discretions without telling you the story of how I very nearly came to be intimately connected to Prince Charles. I had had an innocent teenage holiday romance involving a kiss or two with Anna Wallace, who later became Prince Charles' girlfriend. A couple of years later, just before Anna took up with Prince Charles and consequently went stratospheric with grandness, one dark night in London, I decided to put my oar in, so to speak.

I was walking back from the pub with a mutual friend called Bill Neave at about midnight and I said I did not have a bed for the night. Could he put me up? He said he had no space but Anna Wallace lived nearby and perhaps I could cadge a bed, or at least a sofa, from her. Virginity had now assumed capital letter proportions in my mind, such a burden was it to my sense of self-worth. What was needed was another big word to deal with it and words don't come much bigger than Fate. This is more than coincidence. This is fate, I decided.

We pinged on her doorbell and she very kindly let me sleep on a mattress in her sitting room. There was only a door between me and heaven. I sat up on my mattress and looked at the door that gave off from the sitting room into Anna's bedroom. I looked at that door and that door said: 'Open me'. I was immediately beset by two contradictory clichés: 'Easier said than done' quickly followed by 'Fortune favours the bold'.

Then I thought. 'I am English. I am asphyxiated with inhibition and you cannot just go barging into somebody's bedroom demanding sex. This is too big an ask, and anyway there is the other person to think about. Anna might well not want to have sex with me.' But then I thought: 'She fancied me a couple of years ago. It did not lead to anything sexual because I never took advantage of the situation and anyway my job took me to another distant part of the country. Why shouldn't she still fancy me, I still fancy her?'

And then a thought occurred to me that clinched the deal. 'Put yourself in the other person's shoes. Supposing Anna walked into my bedroom totally naked and asked me to have sex, would I not be delighted? Her lovely curvaceous body is probably right now aching to be covered by my hard and sculpted male form. Her Wallace pussy wants the Fraser dog. She is probably lying there right now, sleepless, thinking: 'Damn that door'. What finally tipped the balance was the niggle: 'You just don't have the guts.'

No door was ever opened more gingerly and I can't say I was naked. I was in shirt and pants. I think I was slightly put off by the fact that she was asleep, but she immediately woke up and said: 'What do you want?' There was a deathly pause and then I spied her wash hand-basin and I said: 'I would like to brush my teeth.' It was very surreal, as excruciating moments invariably are. Time stands still just at the point when you would like it to fast forward. 'Can I borrow your toothbrush?'

Unbelievably she said: 'Yes.'

So I went to the basin and, with my back to her in the bed across the room, I started to brush my teeth. After a time I thought: 'There are only so many teeth I can brush.' Then something made me turn round and say: 'Can I have sex with you?'

'No.'

Jesus, I had not thought of an exit strategy in the event of rejection! How do I get out of this room? She then, I think, felt sorry for me because she said: 'You can kiss me good-night.' So I padded over that long yawning stretch of carpet between the basin and the bed and I gave her a peck on the cheek and then beat a hasty retreat out of the room. The moment I shut the door behind me I performed a physical manoeuvre that I have only ever seen once, since. Basil Fawlty had been humiliated once too often in a particular episode of *Fawlty Towers* and he sort of dropped to his knees while staying on his heels and then he jumped around the room like a demented frog. That is exactly what I did, only silently because Anna was just next door.

I finally got on top of women at university when I realised that the key thing was to stay still. Just don't move. Fright breeds flight or fight. As long as you don't attempt to escape a woman by dashing off or making an excuse or diluting her with other people whom you can hide behind, then you have to engage with her because the fight option is not socially permissible. The effect of staying put for long enough is to calm you down to the level where you can have a proper conversation. That is how I conquered my fear of women.

The Smallest Fraser in the World

I have not been so successful with the working class. Just as I had no contact with girls in the course of my upbringing, so the working class – with all their anarchic and vigorous vitality – was put out of bounds. I was removed from the locality, and all my accented neighbours, at the age of nine, to be turned into a proper little gentleman at my preparatory boarding school.

Not only were those flat Suffolk vowels to be beaten into submission and removed from the lexicon, never to be allowed past my larynx ever again as long as I lived, but they were to be replaced by a tonal but neutral sounding affectation, resident mostly in the nose but also suggesting the placement of two plums in the throat and a silver spoon in the mouth: rendered pitch perfect to make the rest of Britain seethe with resentment until death eventually seals my lips and I'm delivered with relief by working-class coffin bearers to the silence of the grave.

Freedom was to be replaced by discipline, rough by smooth, spontaneity by calculation and ease by formality. To that end, the first thing they did when you entered the hellish portals of prep school was to rob you of your personal identity. In the army they take away your civilian clothes. In a prep school, they take away your Christian name. I was called 'Fraser Minimus', which means the smallest Fraser. There were two bigger ones: Alastair was 'Fraser Major' and Rory, 'Fraser Minor'. My younger brother, Anselm, was lucky. Alastair had left Moreton Hall before he arrived because presumably he would have been called 'Miniscule Fraser'.

Long Live Short-Haired Hippies!

My battle has been with my background. I suppose I was really affected by the much derided hippy movement at the end of the Sixties when I was an impressionable teenager and I thought crass materialism and the class system were going to be dumped in the dustbin of history forever. Progress was once again on the march and it could count on Trooper Fraser (in brackets: Minimus).

But it only took two or three summers of love before the Establishment, amazingly undermined by flower power, closed ranks and re-imposed its authority in the name of normality and bring to an end that wonderful global experiment in communal living. Never mind, it got me hooked and I still see dotted all the over the place, refugees from that period. I call them short-haired hippies and they are currently in their sixties embarking on the final adventure of their lives: old age. And I bet they will do it well because, although they had to compromise with the world of commerce to get married and bring up families, they have all retained a little spirit of that time in the sun. They never took money, power and position seriously. The fellowship of man came first.

My neighbour, sixty-two year-old Richard Harrington is a classic short-haired hippy. (Actually in his case, no-haired hippy because apart from a few strands his mop has gone.) Richard gave up a career as a high flying, Oxbridge educated lawyer to become a sheep farmer an hour's drive North of Inverness. I once asked him whether he did not miss the brilliant, cultural and witty company of highly educated colleagues at work at the Inns of Court and, of course, their super salaries, for the sake of a pittance on the side of a hill and the craic at Dingwall Auction mart.

'I prefer to talk to people who live life rather than talk about it,' was his memorable reply. That put me in my box because, of course, that is all I ever do, but he was really making a point about education which can so easily make you one remove from life.

What I objected to in the culture of my own family were its assumptions. The middle classes are boring. The working classes are simple. You will disappear without money. Life is all about calculation. Their attitude to other people at work is totally exploitative, under a thin veneer of manners and consideration. God is for Sundays, Mammon for the rest of the week. Charm is reserved for the drawing room. A lapse in good taste is a fate worse than death.

Members of my family grade people between higher, lower and equal, depending on where you find yourself on the social pyramid, with a fellow called Lord Lovat perched on the top. Money and beauty will buy you promotion though and sheer naked talent is excused everything. I once introduced my mother to Ted Hughes and she treated him like an equal. A professor of moral philosophy was not so lucky. He was dismissed as 'an interesting little man'. I think I have already referred to my mother's academic career. Glittering is not the first word to spring to mind.

You might be impressed by their apparent self-confidence but really it is the bliss born of ignorance. The key to the British upper classes is that they never dip a toe into anybody else's pool. They keep themselves to themselves. Their relationship to people from the other ranks is purely commercial. No wonder I went down a coalmine for a year.

First Class goes no Faster than Second Class

They thought I was Lord Lucan.

'I don't do moustaches.'

'I bet you do nannies though.'

'Not in the way he did.'

'Oh yeah, he did them in.'

'Only one.'

'Well, that's reassuring!'

The whole thing about the coalmines was having a reply. It was called repartee with the result that the conversation never ended.

Bloody hell, Margaret Thatcher has a lot to answer for, closing down the coalmines: community after community. There were originally 200 mines in Britain and National Union of Miners leader, Arthur Scargill was accused of being outrageously alarmist by the media in 1983 when he claimed that the secret plan was to close 100 of them. He grossly underestimated. I think there are about four left.

I am so glad I decided to go down the pit because I caught the tail end of some important British social history. John Lennon was right. A working-class hero is something to be and I saw lots of them down the pit. They were the old guys who had worked the mines before the advent of modern technology. What we are talking about is the male of the species in all its glory: men with physique, vitality, and culture –T S Eliot's definition of the word. They were powerful men who brooked no nonsense with a quick wit, big character and a good heart. I just imagined one of these guys sitting round a dining room table at home and the automatic respect he would command. They had charisma.

I remember one man in particular, a deputy over-man, Geordie Smith, who could see I was having a hard time of it, with my peer group, on shift. I just wasn't quite strong enough for heavy labour. I would have to stop and rest every dozen or so paces. He got me up to carry a steel girder with him and he took the whole weight of the girder on his shoulder, allowing me virtually to saunter along behind, much to the amazement of the other assembled trainees. His face gave away nothing but, unseen to the others, he gave me the quickest of winks.

The only reason I managed to get a job down the pit was because the government had introduced an early retirement scheme and so many miners had taken advantage of it that they were short staffed and they needed to recruit a few thousand people in a hurry. So, suddenly, there was an influx of trainees, people straight off the street, including myself. My life was made a misery during the month-long training programme. You put a bunch of people together out of nowhere and natural feelings of insecurity will demand a scapegoat. Being the odd one out I was tailor-made for the job. It felt like prep school all over again.

Life got better when we were sent to our individual pits and we were mixed in with the older generation, who enjoyed teasing, baiting and abuse as long as it raised a laugh, but objected to bullying. I stayed a year at Westoe Colliery in South Shields and made a couple of real friends, who came to my wedding a few years later, but I cannot say that I completely conquered my fear of the working class.

My mistake was to treat the escapade like a journalist. I did not fully immerse myself in the experience. I could never banish from my mind my ulterior motive which was to write a book which became *Toff Down Pit* and was marketed as the sequel to *The Road to Wigan Pier*. And I skived off a lot of the actual, quite demanding, physical work required of a transport lad, where you had to load and unload trams with steel girders and wooden chocks, taking materials to the coalface.

That was a big missed opportunity to bond with matter and I would have earned myself a decent physique the right way – not in the gym but down the pit, doing solid graft. I was a fool. I thought only the mind mattered and the only point of the body was to keep the head off the ground. I had not yet read the polemicists and psychologists: Karl Jung, Joseph Campbell or Robert Bly, the author of *Iron John* and novelists: D. H. Lawrence, Ernest Hemmingway, Thomas Hardy, and the guy who wrote *Zorba the Greek*.

What about the Workers?

I want to tell you a story about an amazing train journey I had twenty years later which sums up my feelings about the class system in this country and how I, as a member of the management class, will always be wrong footed by somebody who does the actual work – my natural prejudices confounded by their imagination.

The great thing about British trains is that people don't talk to you. We know the form. You can get an entire coach of up to 100 people being conducted through our green and pleasant land in total silence. Not a single word being said, but you cannot guarantee it. There is such a thing as a foreigner or a salesman or a child and even the occasional person who knows someone and gets all garrulous.

And for that reason we have first class carriages and the tickets are something like twice the price. Of course, these carriages look absolutely identical to the second class carriages, except there is nobody in them and this is the whole point. Alright, their upholstery might be a different colour but there's barely an inch more leg room and the same food and drinks trolley that has served the second class passengers comes through to the first class compartment, and don't think the first class carriage goes any faster than the second class carriage even though it is nearer the engine! No, the real reason why people buy first class tickets is exclusivity.

I remember this one journey back from Aberdeen to Inverness and we picked up passengers at Dyce, where about eight boys from the oil rigs got on. They had not had a drop to drink for a fortnight and nothing to read but porn mags. I don't want to glamorise them but they had been out in the North Sea wrestling with nuts and bolts and standing on iron girders 500 feet in the air and they looked the part. Men with chests and I am not talking bronchial trouble. They wore jeans and tough footwear and they were full to the brim with brilliant wisecracks and you could see the women on the train dismiss them as lager louts.

I quickly pocketed my spent Crunchie wrapper, pulled my tummy in and ground my teeth. I had an empty seat next to me which I was guarding against possible intruders. I sort of messed it up, spread newspapers over it and bundled my jacket on it to give the impression that it was taken by somebody who had only just popped off to the toilet or the buffet car and would be shortly returning. I wouldn't actually lie because that would involve talking. I could just sort of mime that it was taken.

Sitting by himself across the aisle on the other side was this old country priest with a grubby looking habit. He had an old-fashioned face engraved with character. He produced his trusty travelling companion, a battered old bible, cracked it open, sighed, wacked it shut and put it back in his satchel. Then he looked around for entertainment and spotted me making the mistake of looking at him. You could see him thinking for a moment, then he got up and as sure as fate, he came across to me, lent over, peered out of the window and said:

'I was just checking. You see I couldn't tell from where I was sitting and it's a thing I like to get clear before we go much further. It's silly really but I like to know if there's any oncoming traffic. You see, I didn't know if it was single track or, in fact, there was another track just down below where you are and I see that there is.'

I didn't reply. I didn't know how I could.

'Of course,' he said. 'I know exactly what's going on my side of the track and you know what it is like: telegraph wires, yes, nothing but fucking telegraph wires going up and down.'

I thought – did he? – I said: 'Sorry? What did you say?'

'Ha, ha! Question and answer. Excellent! Well now, excuse me. Do you mind if I do or you don't mind if I don't. Well, either way, I will, shall I?' That was the way he asked to sit next to me. 'O aye it's a small world.'

'I am sorry, have we met before?'

He shook his head and said: 'Aye, it could be smaller. But you just never know. It's a funny old thing but there you have it. Sometimes I don't know but then again ever so often sometimes you do. Take my sister, Paddy. She's been courting the same man for the best part of ten years. Now I said to her: 'That's enough courting. It's time you were caught!' Ha. Ha. Ha. Well, at least, I mean well. But that man of hers, just wedded to the idea of being able to provide for her. Funny fucker!' he said, cheerfully shaking his head.

'Are you a priest?'

'Carmelite.'

'I thought that was a silent order.'

'That's right, my son, but you see I'm on holiday.'

'But I mean you're swearing.'

'I was brought up swearing. Where I came from, swearing was like punctuation.' He explained. 'It's great just to let off steam on holiday.'

'But I mean, isn't it sort of immoral?' was my prissy response.

'Jesus Christ himself was working-class. Do you think he minded his p's and q's?'

Alright, I confess. I made up that last exchange in a prayer. I was using my imagination. That is permissible in this book as you will discover later.

You can't Beat Darwin

My intellectual inferiority complex was equally difficult to put to bed. I co-founded a residential writers' centre with my sister, Sophia. I designed a week-long residential course called: 'How To Be An Intellectual In A Week' and I married the brainiest girl at university, which I attended at the late age of twenty-six. I was so determined to slay the dragon of inarticulation that I was happy to interrupt my nascent journalistic career at a point when it might have led to a serious job in London.

I got a dismal 2/2. I was sacked as the chairman of the writers' centre for my administrative incompetence. I took my own course, specially designed to relieve feelings of mental inadequacy, and failed to feel like an intellectual at the end of it and my wife left me because, amongst other reasons, I wasn't clever enough for her. My thought-to-word capability was insufficient. But there were compensations, mainly my four children. I very selflessly mixed my gene pool with my wife's and without giving Darwin too much credit, I can say that evolution has not failed the little nippers. They are effortlessly brighter than their father. They have a natural God-given eloquence for which I would give my back teeth.

Obviously, I am still a work in progress battling against my fears and pursuing my desires but that is the story to date of my individual struggle for self-expression. My first book in this trilogy, *The Spiritual Diet*, was about my personal pursuit of goodness, truth and beauty hence my immersion in God, nature and poetry. My second book, *The Joy of Talk*, was about trying to overcome my intellectual shortcomings and providing myself with the wherewithal to conduct a successful intimate relationship through the only means available to man, which is talk. My broken marriage is testimony to the fact that my efforts have not been met with universal success but life is all in the attempt. This book concerning old age is about community, crashing through all social barriers, including class. Old age is the great leveller.

This book also helps me put into context my personal journey through life. Old age gives one perspective. 'In the autumn of your life, your experience is harvested. This is a backdrop against which we can understand ageing. Ageing also invites you to become aware of the sacred circle that shelters your life. Within the harvest circle, you are able to gather lost moments and experiences, bring them together and hold them as one. In actual fact, if you can come to see ageing not as the demise of your body, but as the harvest of your soul, you will learn that ageing can be a time of great strength, poise and confidence.' writes John O'Donohue in his masterpiece, *Anam Cara*.

CHAPTER SEVEN

Learning to be a Part

Nobody wants to be alone. We need padding, and life naturally provides that up until the point of old age. The most effective padding you can get is a nice, fleshy person or two or twenty, or maybe more if you happen to need a lot of reassurance. Some people are crazy for social popularity and even more extreme cases are not even satisfied until they are famous, known and loved by millions.

At the most primitive level padding is actually a physical thing, which is one of the reasons why boys at school rough and tumble with one another and girls go round arm in arm, and it explains all sport. And then you have children of your own and you like them to sprawl all over you and then of course you have a wife whom you clamber on top of at the end of a long day and sometimes she likes to climb aboard your own good self. Why not? It all helps to remind you that you exist and it keeps nothingness at bay.

It is also a metaphorical thing. You want to feel there is somebody beneath you and promotion at work offers you that feeling. The best thing about promotion is not that it gets you nearer to the top, which is an abstract; it is that it puts people underneath you and that is practically physical.

In your social life you want to feel surrounded by friends. It is the void you are fighting physically and mentally. You need to put people between you and emptiness.

The beauty of community is that it corrals people into a given place and so it gives you the lovely feeling of being surrounded. Unfortunately technology has so weakened the sense of belonging in a neighbourhood, like a village or a town or a city district, that we are left hanging onto, and feeling terribly nostalgic after retirement for the world of work, which offered us the regular contact with other people that we naturally crave.

Old age casts you out of that Garden of Eden, which might have felt like a jungle at the time, but as with all earthly paradises you only fully appreciate it after you have been banished. Now you are out on a limb and you are left to your own devices. Your job now is to recreate community for yourself. There is no other way of ageing successfully. Your community life so far has gone: family, school, university, office, grass.

Man enters and departs this world on his own and in recognition of that solitary fact, a man should learn to spend time profitably by himself, engaged in prayer. He should take part in creative activity, either receiving or producing art of one form or another, and finally he should commune with nature. Then he feels like a three dimensional person.

Secondly, a man finds sustenance in relationships with his fellow men on a one-to-one basis. This produces feelings of love and/or friendship. And, finally, he needs to situate himself within the body of a community to which he attaches himself and is rewarded with a sense of belonging. It makes him feel grounded.

Old age greatly strengthens your sense of solitude and affords a wonderful opportunity to develop yourself in that respect. It not only gives you the inclination as the great philosophic questions, the eternal verities, now become genuine subjects of contemplation as the prospect of death approaches, but also you are afforded the acres of time needed to immerse yourself in these solitary imaginings.

However, you can't help feel that your ties to other people loosen, reflecting the inescapable fact that you are becoming increasingly less important to the people around you. Feelings become less intense. Obviously people no longer fall in love with you. Wrinkles preclude that phenomenon. Friendships just potter along or dwindle away to a gentle mutual regard.

The problem with old age is the distance it puts between you and the centre of things. Where once you were king of your household, sitting at the top of the table as your children clamoured for your attention, and even your wife, because you were the only other adult in the room, now there is silence because everybody has gone.

Now your children have got their own domains complete with circling wives and children. You have now got to get used to having slipped down the rankings. You are your precious daughter's fifth favourite person in the world and quite frankly your wife's least favourite person, because she has gone and sugared off with somebody else and you are now the enemy and those still with spouses can so easily merely co-exist. Thank God for the exceptions, but this book addresses the majority of us.

Your social clout has been severely dented because the craic has dropped down a generation. The action is elsewhere. You have become a bit of an obligation.

Here starts the fight-back. I know humility is the finest Christian virtue but come on, have some pride. First, you have got to acclimatise yourself to the new reality and come to terms with your various demotions in other people's esteem. You have got to learn the most difficult lesson of old age. You have to learn to become part of the furniture. So it goes: chair, table, lampstand, granddad. Instead of dominating proceedings, you have now got to learn to be happy just to be part of them.

Take my eighty-seven year-old mother, for example. She is what they call in Brixton 'old school'. She is a daughter of Empire – the sort of person you could in colonial times fire off into the Congo with an umbrella for the monsoon (OK, wrong country, but who's counting?) and a bottle of quinine to deal with malaria and she would maintain standards despite tribal differences of opinion. Tea is served on the verandah at four-thirty with cucumber sandwiches even if the servants are going down with smallpox. 'Just tell them not to breathe over the cake.'

It is that indomitable spirit that has stood her in good stead in her old age. She was widowed twenty years ago. My ex-wife and myself and my sister-in-law were all writing books last year. So there was a certain amount of literary chat and this planted a seed in my mother's mind. She thought she would write one herself.

Most people would be quite daunted by the monumental task of writing one's first book at the age of eighty-six without ever having committed pen to paper professionally before in her life and indeed without even having noticeably benefited from education at all. She completed, I think, a total of two years at school; her early years having been tutored by a German governess who, apart from imparting an appreciation of Hitler, spent a lot of time appraising sentimental Victorian poetry. I think Mum got a smattering of what was called standard grades, but the equivalent of A-levels proved a bridge too far.

A couple of years later I met a friend of mine, James Gibbs, in the street in Inverness and he said: 'Kit, all is well with the world again. I know we are deep in a recession and my jobs hangs by a thread, the woman I want to marry has postponed me another year and standards are collapsing all around us, but then I got your mother's invitation to her book launch!'

'And?'

'Well, I mean to say, how can you resist it? Obviously book launches are to be avoided at all cost but not this one! Not your mother's book with a title like: *Second World War Memorials in the Highlands and Other Significant Monuments.*' He roared with laughter. 'That's quality.'

That's all he said but I know what had charmed him. He loved the modesty of her endeavour and its plain homage to the unsung heroes of her youth, the sheer locality of her research and that fabulously cumbersome title of no commercial appeal at all. All this ran so contrary to the horribly aspirant world of today where nobody puts pen to paper without secretly nurturing absurd dreams of fame and wealth.

My mother had got round the problem of not having any literary talent as such, let alone the necessary education and ability to form a sentence lengthy enough to accommodate a clause and, perish the thought, a sub-you-know clause. She merely went around the Highlands photographing war memorials and copying down what was inscribed on the stones and then she padded it out with relevant stuff off the internet and other sources of information. She got her nephew-in-law, who has a print works, to print a few hundred copies at a reduced price and then got a few hundred of her extended family to buy a few copies each to pay the nephew-in-law. She did not marry into a family of six, and have six children of her own for nothing, all of whom are perfectly capable of breeding for themselves. If you can't write a bestseller, you can at least breed readers.

I remember one expedition in particular where she lured half a dozen assorted members of her family into her car with what she said was merely 'a quick whiz round the North of Scotland'. She wanted company on a trip to bag yet more memorials on the way to Cape Wrath and the island beyond. She realised she would probably need help over fences and then there was that boat trip at the end which would need negotiating. One of the grandchildren very quickly felt car sick and so changed places with my mother in the front seat, so she travelled the 150 miles to Cape Wrath crammed in the back. The boat ride to the island was over what they call choppy waters, then a brief yomp over one and a half hills to get to the war memorial she coveted.

She nobbled another couple of war memorials on the journey back and unbeknownst to everybody including herself, had a stroke squashed in the back of the car. She probably did not have enough room to flail about the place, as is normally what happens with a stroke, so everyone is excused blame for not noticing.

The other theory is that all the fresh air she had imbibed in the course of the day had knocked her out, so perhaps she had the stroke in her sleep. It was obviously a relatively minor one because it did not stop her helping her two daughters cook for 16 people for dinner, a not unusual number of people on our family's fortnight summer holidays. Over dinner, people thought she had mistakenly drunk too much because she had been slurring her words.

Overnight, she had another stroke but, unbelievably, that did not stop her making breakfast which normally happens in shifts with young mothers up first with their toddlers and hung over adolescents getting their eggs and bacon in just before the lunch shift. That day two of the nephews were the first to breakfast because they had got up early to stalk roe deer. They did not even notice that their grandmother's face was skew-whiff but, in their defence, they were starving and distracted by the huge fry up she served them.

It took my sister, Sophia, who came in next for breakfast, to realise what had happened and she showed Mum her face in the mirror who burst into tears at the shock of it. I am glad to report that she very quickly recovered in hospital and afterwards, in convalescence, from the strokes.

I am just giving you a flavour of the woman. It is a portrait of an old woman negotiating age with all the qualities you need to enjoy the thing. In this context she is our role model.

When I was a young man she was my ideological enemy. To me she represented convention. She believed in outward appearance although she would dismiss brilliant socialites as 'silly women'. She was a champion of normality. 'Prayer does not really work,' she once confided in me, 'but it is a nice thing to do.' She upheld the social order. 'People should be kept in their place for their own good. Otherwise it is like living abroad – fun for a short while but very quickly you want to go home.' And she was a big proponent of what I call 'should' and 'ought', whereas I believe in 'is'. So with her, if something should be a certain way, it is that way. Happiness is just an exercise of will. Also she was a fifties woman, with all that that entails. Her classic refrain, which she uttered with great pride, was that men had bigger brains than women.

But now I myself am older I am not distracted by her opinions. Instead I can appreciate her qualities like her incredible stoicism and her sense of adventure. She just says 'yes' to everything, no matter what the invitation, no matter what the inconvenience. Next week she is going on a tour with a choir to Germany. She does not know anybody in the choir except her son-in-law, Joshua Vanneck, who was himself widowed last year and he will spend most of his time busy socialising with everybody else in the group. She will be older than anybody else by a margin of at least twenty years and she doesn't sing a note.

She will just be sitting happily in the background absorbing the atmosphere and silently enjoying the change of scenery. She has great personal dignity, a poise born of the unfeigned natural snobbery of her age where she was brought up to think she was better than other people because she occupied a position, bequeathed at birth, further up the social scale and she has seen no reason to question this absurd prejudice. It has suited her just fine and given her a little lift throughout her life in her dealings with others. And the end result? A false self-confidence maybe, but certainly better than no self-confidence at all.

However she has come about it, she has arrived at the enviable position of being able to cope with a lack of attention which for all my enlightened and egalitarian opinions, I do not share. So it is no problem for her if she is not spoken to for an hour here or two on her trip to Germany with Joshua's choir; she won't for one moment feel left out of things – she will feel part of them.

She has also had good training at playing second fiddle, having been married to an immensely charismatic man, and she is used to being sidelined by her family of six voracious offsprings competing aggressively for attention between themselves. She has learnt the art of selfless enjoyment, essential for old age, and I am currently studying her closely.

Routine Giveth and Routine Taketh Away

Old people can tip over the edge. They can get wiped off the map of regular human contact. That is why community is so important for them and if it is not made obviously available, you just have to carve out your own personal territory. You have got to make your own daily round – like a visit to the pub at such and such a time for one and a half drinks and a knocking on the door of some other old bugger who hasn't seen a human himself for a couple of days, except on the TV. You need to be as pushy as a salesman. If the world won't come to you, you have got to go to it.

In this big empty universe you have to fend for yourself, otherwise you will sink beneath the waters of other people's complete in-difference and drown in a sea of your own loneliness and despair.

'No, this is not going to happen to me,' you need to say for yourself. 'I am going to make a success of the last third of my life. I have done youth and I scored 62 per cent, middle age fouled up at the end and I lost some valuable percentage points. I want to end on a high. Most people tail off and ruin their overall life score. So this is where I am going to jolly well major, surprise the world with a high score. O yes!'

I strongly recommend spending disproportionate money on clothes so when you step out of a day in search of human contact, people will look at you and say: 'He looks dapper. Here is a man who turns himself out well, kitted out in good cloth with a little flourish like a buttonhole and maybe a Trilby on the nut.'

A tie always looks good on an old man. It shows you are maintaining discipline to the very end. You are quintessentially not letting yourself go. Everybody else in their witless youth and easy middle age can afford to cut themselves some slack but to success-fully get through the last quadrant of life you need to toughen up because you are going to be attacked at any moment by illness and a thousand other frailties.

Why is community so important that you should allow it control over your life? You have no choice. Whether you like it or not, it determines the way you think. It doesn't matter whether you are enslaved to its mores or sit in permanent opposition or whether your attitude lies somewhere in between these two extremes – what you are responding to is convention: group thinking.

You can lock yourself away in isolated seclusion and delve deep into scholarship, cut yourself off from the world and think alone in your ivory tower, the solitary genius of private thought. That is your time in the desert but there will come a moment when you will want to bring the fruits of your intellectual endeavour to the market place, because ultimately man is a creature of communication and you cannot deny your nature. You know that before you first disappear into your library and it will colour your thinking for the entire time of any self-imposed study.

So nobody is immune to society, especially not the old who at the drop of a hat can be bundled off into some hellish institution like a hospital or an old people's home. Institutions are the fixed assets of society and all those who work in them are the moving parts.

You can say goodbye to privacy and all the rights of man. You will be treated like a moron by people who in your prime would be opening doors for you and begging favours. 'How are we doing today? Have we done a poo?' (The answer to that is: 'I have. Have you?')

All you are left with is your own personal dignity, which is why I recommend cultivating a strict dress code. The first thing they take away from you when you join an institution like prison or the army is your wardrobe. Top of the shopping list: silk pyjamas. Show the bastards you are quality.

Yes, in old age you need to respect society because it not only provides you with the environment in which you can make for yourself a decent daily routine if you are outgoing, and even if you are not, you have got to make yourself that way, but you should fear it too because it can imprison you in the long, boring, painful lead up to death.

Without community there is nothing. That is alright for the young and the middle aged who are busy at work or at school and come home to a family, but an old man not only comes home to nothing, he does not go out to anything either. He is alone in the darkness – nothing but him and the kettle.

Where would an Englishman be without his comforting cup of tea? I remember when my sixty-eight year-old father died, as far as I was concerned quite unnecessarily, in Raigmore hospital in Inverness. He had spent the whole day fighting desperately for his life.

He had had a bad heart attack, not that I have ever seen a good one, on the Sunday and he had been rudely awoken on the Tuesday with another one. Monday he had spent flirting with the nurses, accusing them all of being twenty-three.

We had been by his bedside throughout Tuesday while he was close-eyed on the borderline of consciousness, my mother asking him how he felt: 'Bloody awful,' and him on one occasion feeling her hands with his hands. That physical enquiry turned out to be their last communication.

And then in came a couple of nurses at 6.20 p.m. saying that they had to change his bed linen. 'No, no, surely not. He is busy. He is fully occupied trying to save his life. I wouldn't disturb him. He needs all his energy for the job at hand.' I thought. But you never say these things at the time because you are merely a solitary in-dividual equipped only with a paltry little thing like common sense and they are the experts. That is why they are in white coats. They know what they are doing and anyway there is a hospital to run with rules to obey.

We were asked to leave the room so that they could change his sheets and they managed to kill him in ooh 2 minutes. In only a few seconds alarm bells rung and a lot of doctors and nurses came rushing down corridors into the intensive care ward and then after a couple of minutes they all came trooping out studiously avoiding our anxious, questioning eyes.

But it was all OK because we were immediately offered a cup of tea. Somebody dying is so shocking that the only thing you can say in the immediate aftermath is: 'Do you want a cup of tea?' And if you are British, you will find yourself saying: 'Yes please. Mine's with milk and two sugars.'

When was the Last Time you saw a Woman Swoon?

The power of the group can sweep all before it with common sense being the first thing that goes overboard, closely followed by consideration of others. I saw a TV documentary presented by the actor and comedian Alan Davies celebrating that unfashionable decade, the Seventies, whose great achievement was the social revolution that eventually brought about the equality of the sexes. He was reminiscing about his time at the University of Kent and how hugely affected students had been by the publication of Germaine Greer's *The Female Eunuch*.

This is the first generation of feminists who were so fierce in their revolutionary passion to right the wrongs of centuries of male chauvinism that they ended up actually disliking men themselves. He said, personally speaking, it was quite frustrating because so many attractive female students who would otherwise have been potential girlfriends put themselves out of bounds by becoming lesbian. He said that the initial revolutionary fervour wore off, they reverted to heterosexuality but in the meantime, it was lean pickings for your average young male predator. That is the real demonstration of the power of group thinking. It can even change your sexuality.

Now, go back to the Victorian era where it was the norm for women to swoon in drawing rooms. Why the hell don't women swoon any more? Where are the smelling salts these days? Can you imagine being a Victorian woman and having to faint every time you hear or see something inappropriate? They can't all have been faking it. Social conditioning is that powerful it can rob you of your consciousness.

I don't for one moment feel superior to these collapsing women. I, personally, was brainwashed into thinking that being sent away to school at the age of seven was perfectly normal and I was being held back in my development because, unlike most of my contemporaries, I was being kept at home until the comparatively later age of nine. There was a memorable scene in the film *Billy Elliot*, showing the hero's elder brother's reaction to Billy's ballet teacher's proposal to get him to audition for a place at the Royal Ballet School, which was a boarding school.

'You're not taking him away! He's only a bairn. What about giving him a childhood?! exclaimed the older brother.

What my class thought was a privilege, for which they would pay handsomely, the working class saw as something deeply damaging and frankly downright cruel. And *Billy Elliot* was the ripe old age of eleven!

Consensus can go either way. In the political context it is at its best when moderated by precedent and kept in check by democracy. The store of suffering over decades gives rise to a universal desire not to repeat historic mistakes and elections give the people a periodic opportunity to keep government on course to deliver progress.

Where consensus goes wrong is in the time of social upheaval and financial collapse when a people go collectively mad, and we all know the case in point. Unfortunately, it looks as if we could be approaching that time again but we will surely have learnt from the last time.

Wherever you get two or three people gathered together in the name of anything, we all know absurd behaviour is just around the corner but we also know that, laborious, bureaucratic and cumbersome though the method of expression and means of action, an individual is lost without belong to a group or number of groups.

From playgroup power struggles to Catholic Church cover-ups, all totally unnecessary and completely counter-productive though they might be, I would nevertheless not like to be a mother of a toddler without a playgroup or a spiritual person without a church. Left to your own devices, you get into so much trouble because you have no means of comparison by which you can judge what society regards as normal.

Normal might be nuts but, at least, you are not by yourself. Listen to what G. K. Chesterton famously said about people who abandon church: 'It is not that non-believers suddenly start believing in nothing, they believe in anything.' Just look at all those crazy people who believe in the power of crystals or where the bloody stars are in the heaven. Millions of people, in all seriousness, believe in astrology and you don't want to enquire too deeply into Scientology.

First World War officers had to wear moustaches which made it easy for German snipers to distinguish them from the rank and file and pick them off at their leisure. That barmy army regulation was the product of group thinking. A large organisation is basically a herd and it has that kind of mentality. There is a huge consensus which you go against at your peril. You go against it and you won't get promoted.

Old Age can give you the Detachment not to be Swept Up in the Latest Pieties

Committee rules and it results in a million madnesses proliferated by the idiocy of bureaucracy, but what makes it worse half the time are the original strategic decisions that spawn the thousands of other lesser decisions cascading down the hierarchy of command until you finally arrive at chestnut trees in Norfolk having to be cut down in case a conker falls on a toddler's head. We have to thank Health and Safety for that piece of zealotry.

The power of the group, whose absurd pieties necessarily abound as people fall over one another in their desperate desire to conform, can make policy decisions of such startling stupidity it would astonish a primary school kid. The more the power the greater the conformity and the nuttier the consensus and we don't need to look any further than at ourselves over the last few years. The Subprime Property Scandal showed the entire banking industry lending money to people who could not possibly pay them back, making a mountain of toxic debt inevitable and the Derivatives' scandal saw them taking part in pyramid selling on a global scale, which we all know ends in empty pockets. Bankers' justification for their massive bonuses is that they are financial geniuses. You can't make it up!

Look at the utter absurdity of the convention that underarm deodorant sprays caused a hole in the ozone layer. One look at the size of a deodorant can, one glance at the hugeness of the sky, let alone space beyond it and you don't have to be a science major – to be American for a moment – to realise the nonsense of that particular alarm. . No one talks about the hole in the ozone layer any more because it has gone. Obviously Right Guard Roll-on saved the day! Yeh, right.

And what about those little, pooping power station chimneys issuing forth tiny strands of smoke. You almost feel sorry for them. The work they have to do to heat up the whole of the world. Obviously it is balderdash which is why the scientific community had to surreptitiously airbrush the words 'Global Warming' from our communal memories because over the last couple of decades since their dire warnings, the world has obstinately refused to warm up. And they have replaced it with the absolutely inspired term: 'Climate Change' because, of course, no two years' weather is ever the same. This time they can never be wrong.

And anyway I don't see what the panic is about. Our weather system has done hot and cold before. It was hot enough in Roman times for there to be vineyards around York, and cold enough in the Elizabethan era to skate on the Thames and even if there was something in the current thinking, there's nothing we can do about it because man-made emissions only account for five per cent of the total output.

And as for the Euro – a doomed currency for the obvious reason that Southern European nations don't want to work half as hard as Northern European nations because of their climate.

CJD was confidently predicted to kill 100,000 of us. I think the actual number was closer to 67. And of all the rain that has fallen on my head in the last thirty years, not one drop has proven to be acidic and I have lived in a country famous for its rain. All the flus, whether they be pig- or bird- have proven to be damp squibs. We have even failed to be ravaged by AIDS. It is all group hysteria.

The solution is that just because you take part in the group, you do not have to abide by their thinking. You must always think for yourself and in old age you have got plenty of time to carry out your research and come to your own conclusions. Here is a test to see if you think for yourself. What do you think of America, the Champion of the West, in relation to its behaviour in the East? What do you think of the citizens of North Korea? I will answer those two questions without pandering to public opinion. Trip me up only if you can spot a hole in my argument.

I have got nothing against America. It might get things wrong but it is basically well intentioned, as you would expect from a big, ignorant, greedy but very Christian country. It rescued the world twice in the last century and eventually got the better of the Soviet Union by spending them into bankruptcy through the cunning ruse of challenging them to an arms race they could not afford. The result of this successful, much derided, policy was to liberate Eastern Europe from the Soviet yoke. Also to its credit, America, as usual ably abetted by the UK, rescued Bosnia from Serbian aggression when the rest of the Islamic world did not lift a finger for their fellow Muslims and for those critics who say America does nothing for anybody without an ulterior motive, I would dare to mention that there is not a drop of oil in what used to be called Yugoslavia. That's the near East dealt with.

America has tried to export democracy to the Middle East not without some degree of success. After a couple of wars they replaced a tyrant with a democracy in Iraq and, unsurprisingly, that led to the Arab Spring. Of course, progress is two steps forward one step back and so imperfect are these fledgling democracies that they have got a long and troublesome journey before they finally arrive at our current stable and equitable styles of administration in the West. It took us centuries to get it right and it will take them time too but the wait is worth it.

America's intentions were to liberate the people of Afghanistan and Iraq from fundamentally Fascist regimes and they have not totally failed. Iraq was purging, genociding and invading and now it is just involved in comparatively low level, inter-religious, sectarian crossfire and so the body count has gone right down. Afghanistan is currently, to a large extent, not run by the Taliban, which has got to be a bonus.

America's record in the Far East, on the other hand, has not been so impressive. Vietnam was a mistake. It was a failure. And Korea was a war crime. It was genocide – no other word to describe it. In a very cowardly fashion the Americans got into their myriad aeroplanes and from an unassailable height dropped a billion bombs and flattened a country, killing 4 million people in the process.

We are all brainwashed. We are brainwashed into thinking America is a big, bad bully – irrespective of its chequered history, as summarised above. We think there is nothing wrong with drugs and pornography as long as we consume them in moderation. We think it is perfectly acceptable to spend most of our leisure time sitting comatose in front of the television, the internet and the play station. We cannot conceive of socialising without recourse to alcohol and we treat sex like a commodity and we have been conditioned to think that ultimately the only thing that matters at work is money. People come second to Pounds. These are the predominant views in the West.

And we laugh at the people in North Korea for being brainwashed. I saw a 2003 documentary on television following the footsteps of two young schoolgirls over a period of a year as they trained and prepared to take part in the celebrations for the annual mass games in honour of their President.

It reassured me to see the classic communist cityscape of rows of hellish semi-derelict tower blocks and some pretty shoddy-looking roads and pavements. I was glad to see cracks and potholes. Concrete, concrete everywhere, an inner city sink. Then we peer into their little apartment flats and it is as basic as you can get. There were no extras, just rudimentary sticks of furniture. There were no luxuries. The state guaranteed everything including enough jobs, food, housing and education for everyone. Can you imagine? These people have no money worries. There is no mortgage. There is no rent and yes, there's probably no car but what do you need a car for when you are not allowed to go anywhere without permission, which takes half a day of queuing and filling in forms?

The scourge of unemployment does not touch North Korea. Everybody is occupied one way or another. They spend 200 million man hours training for the annual mass synchronised gymnastic spectacular, for example. It puts the opening ceremony of the Olympic Games into the shade and they do this every year. Freed of the tyranny of the profit motive, the state can do what it wants with the labour of its people. I was reminded of Ancient Egypt with Kim Il Sung as a pharaoh.

To be honest, I prefer a pyramid to the bonfire of gadgets and baubles and trinkets that we in the West produce to distract ourselves from anything serious. What North Korea does is weapons and games. This poxy, wee country has got nuclear bombs and Mass Games: 80,000 people in one dance and nobody putting a toe out of line and million strong march pasts. Our two schoolgirls were involved in a dance sequence that involved a certain amount of throwing, catching, rolling and trapping of red rubber footballs. There must have been 5,000 schoolgirls employed in the sequence. Not one ball was dropped or went astray and one of the moves included catching a ball behind your back and all balls had to be doing the same thing at the same time.

What they don't have in North Korea, apart from prosperity, is our much vaunted freedom of expression. Their television broadcasts a mixture of party propaganda and bad movies. It is only available five hours a day and it is so boring it does not encourage viewing. They have been given a secular religion with Kim Il Sung as God and America as the Devil. Their devotion to the Great Leader appears genuine, especially with the children. Their hatred of America is definitely real but then ignorance always lends itself more easily to hatred than to love.

Now, here is the extraordinary thing and here the television cannot dissemble. Unlike us with our annual consumption of 50 million prescriptions of anti-depressants in the UK, North Koreans are happy. You can tell from their shy smiles and their suppressed laughter never far away from conversation. Their lightness of spirit and the frugality of their lifestyles remind me of monks and nuns and just like their religious confreres they are asked for the duration of their task to surrender their individuality, their capricious little egos for the greater good and the greater glory of their God, which in their case happens to be a fat dumpling called Kim Il Jung.

We in the West labour under the cult of the individual as well but with us the individual is ourselves. This is best illustrated in TV shows like *X Factor* and *Britain's Got Talent* where the crass exhibitionism and absurd egotism of nearly all the performers compare unfavourably with the charm and humility of the people taking part in North Korean Mass Games, where tens of thousands perform great gymnastic displays of skill and artistry as if they were one person. Of course, the sense of belonging they must get from the self-surrender to the needs of the group is probably sufficient reward. Self-forgetfulness is practically a dictionary definition of happiness. Surrender of the ego is victory of the soul.

In the midst of abstinence, the simplest thing is an object of desire. 'I miss my sister but now she has gone to the army, I get her room,' says one of the girls with a mischievous smile. The room is like a generous cupboard. They have beautiful manners and show great courtesy to one another and they have tremendous respect for their elders. The surviving grandmother is not farmed out to old peoples' home but is very much part of the family.

They are such an innocent people. What a contrast to the regime that oppresses them. It is so corrupt. We, of course, are the reverse. Our governments are comparatively innocent and we privately behave abominably – gross in our consumption, indifferent to the marvels of nature that surround us and impossible to impress other than by special effect. Now see how well we behave in public, scrutinised as we are by the ravenous press. Our parliamentary expenses scandal was sweet. The MPs were covertly encouraged to claim generously for themselves, to compensate for the fact that no successive government dare offer themselves parallel pay rises in time of high inflation because they had to be showing the nation an example. So salaries fell badly behind those of their equivalent in industry and finance. As it was, the fiddles were tiny. One MP even claimed for a bath plug. My brother's brother-in-law was crucified for a flat screen TV. And as for poor Chris Huhne, the LibDem energy minister, we sent him to prison for a motoring offence. O dear old me, he lied! Who wouldn't palm off a few points on to a reluctant wife to save his car licence? I tried to do it myself, although the old hound went all moral on me and refused to comply, which I thought was a bit rich considering her track record in other affairs.

Later in the documentary we see the two girls thrilled to be taken on a rare outing in the country. We know from Jane Austen novels that when very little happens, your senses are honed to such a pitch of appreciation that the slightest departure from the norm can send you into raptures of delight. The girls are taken to Mount Somethingorother which has a lake cradled in its body burrowed out by previous volcanic eruption. The girls are transported by a sense of awe and wonder. One of them says she feels like the daughter of the mountain. I prefer her enthusiasm to Ronald Reagan's reaction to the sight of the Great Wall of China. 'When you've seen one wall, you've seen them all.' he said. Enthusiasm comes from the Greek word: *theos* which means God. Enthusiasm means having put God into something.

North Korea proves two things particularly relevant to people entering old age. It proves the benefits of surrendering yourself to the group and the spiritual nature of happiness which can occur in reduced circumstances. Monasteries are based on that principle. When he was Abbot of Ampleforth, Cardinal Basil Hume told his novices training to be monks to expect to be happy. That is a fruit of successful spiritual endeavour. Pleasure, the pursuit of which we in the West devote our working lives, is physical and, yes, money can buy it. Old age sees a decline in the opportunity and experience of physical pleasure, so we might as well start pursuing happiness. That involves spiritual discipline.

CHAPTER EIGHT

Time is on your Side

What is culture? I have noted in my diary, a twenty-five year-old American back-packer told me how much she enjoyed the Brixton Bookjam, an event a local self-published novelist had put on in our pub, where about a dozen writers read an extract or two from their works and then a rather ramshackle discussion took place from the stage. Most of the people had been published and it created a little buzz with a good one hundred people in attendance.

Her exact quote was: 'I've come to Europe to get some culture. There is none in America. I've come to listen and learn. I heard some good stuff tonight.' I was charmed by her modesty and her openness, but I think she was looking in the wrong direction.

Culture is what I found in France, which I proceeded to record in my diary giving my personal top ten encounters during a fortnight's holiday.

1) *Boules de Mais Enrobe de Miel* otherwise known as the cereal: Cornpops.
2) The superiority complex of the French. The French campsite staff won't socialise or even deign to associate with the happy-go-lucky English holiday reps. I saw one holiday rep quaking in front of an impeccable campsite officer asking on my behalf whether she would contact the telephone operator for me for a reverse charge call.
3) 'Do you take MasterCard?'
   'No.'
   'But what is that MasterCard sign on the window then?'

'Oh, MasterCard! Yes, of course, we take MasterCard.'

4) The female French bank-teller, beautifully coiffured with gold jewellery and perfectly tailored dress, looking as if she was a Bond Street art gallery owner. Hardly any customers in the bank as if not the done thing, certainly discouraged: two locked doors to get in, button to press for entry, released by staff inside.

5) Flowers in the cemetery. Every grave had flowers, as if their occupants had only died last week.

6) Amazing how anybody serving you had a smile for you while at the same time always retaining their air of cultural superiority. Same as the Gaels in the Highlands, only with them you don't get the smile. They don't waste them on cultural gentiles, especially not Sassenachs.

7) Because France doesn't share the same language as America, the French are still formal and traditional in the way they speak. Its people have impeccable manners, a curiosity and seamless conversation, an enviable attention to the present and spotless public urinals without a word of graffiti. Thankfully, they are saved by their execrable pop music, hopeless TV and 1950s style of advertising.

8) They do chic not cool.
They are born middle-aged.
The Greeks are born old.
The Yanks and Brits do youth and then fall away sharply.

9) No bags at the supermarket counter. They refuse to recognise the prospect of anybody being so coarse as to buy in bulk. It runs completely contrary to their culture which recommends refinement. Gourmet not gourmand.

10) French for free range chicken is *poulets éleve de liberté*. I fully expected them to have added the words: '*égalité et fraternité*'. It's as if even the chickens are politically aware.

Culture is the effect of group thinking. As Toilets himself said, culture is not books, plays, poems and films, as my American back-packer imagined. They are cultural products. T. S. Eliot argued that writers of integrity are merely the channel through which a people's experience, in all its myriad variety, is best expressed. A great writer is a pure syphon.

So, not even Shakespeare is culture. Only the concentrate of his work that became part of our general consciousness is culture: that which unwittingly affected our manner of speech and general outlook. Initially what he wrote came out of the life and times of the people around him in that part of the UK. He did not invent the English language and the way it was spoken in the late sixteenth and early seventeenth century. That was formed by UK society at large.

What Shakespeare did was tap into a pool of references made available to people at the time informed by the classics, the rough and tumble of street talk, the world of agriculture and trade, war and diplomacy, play and work, love, sex, scholarship – all the activities that occupied people at the time. There was no language of technology or rocket science or even heavy industry because none of it had been invented. Shakespeare, for all his genius, could not escape his time or his place. He just brilliantly cobbled together everything that was available to him. Art is pastiche of experiences past and present. It is circumscribed by community.

What an artist does is dip into the pool of references that we, in a particular culture, all share, select a variety of items and juxtapose them in such a way that it amuses and interests us. A word is just a reference point. It is a label. It is just a noise that carries a payload of meaning that we as a group have agreed on between ourselves through the workings of precedent.

You put one word next to another one and it creates an effect. It is a little bit of magic. It is what happens when the sum of the parts is greater than the elements that separately make up the whole. At some point some clever dick a few decades ago, for example, put the word: 'anally' next to the word 'retentive' and created a memorable truthful but funny phrase to describe a stingy person. It gave it a scientific gloss while drumming up lavatorial connotations. It made it possible to insult somebody while apparently being impartial. That is a little bit of artistry.

Culture is consensus. It is sort of unspoken. It is an understanding by society. The culture of the time between the wars, for example, was racist. In Western Europe it was basically accepted that black people were inferior to white people and, of course, Jews were not thought much of either. Read somebody who was considered one of the great writers of his era, Somerset Maugham. One of his masterpieces was a based on the life of the artist Paul Gauguin: *The Moon and Sixpence.* Here is a quote from the book: 'You know how natives love to herd together.' Second World War hero, Wing Commander Guy Gibson had a much loved black dog called 'Nigger', immortalised in the film *The Dam Busters* which was all quite normal and acceptable at the time.

Of course, you have pioneers of the human race: exceptional people – primarily philosophers who question the fundamental precepts of society – but they are not part of culture. They are astronauts really. Intellectually speaking, they have left planet Earth. They are circling the globe: seeking new worlds in which they map out new territory. Whatever they find, they bring back in their metaphorical rockets and what we do is, as Gandhi says, is: 'First ignore them, then laugh at them, then fight them, then accept them.' and the final victory is to absorb them in our language.

Great writers and thinkers increase our stock of references, increase our communal understanding. Freud was a huge contributor. He has given us words like 'complex', 'inhibition' and 'ego'. He wrote treatises explaining and proving to our satisfaction the new power of these words, the new slants he gave them and then we used the words in the way that he taught us to use them. He even taught us how to use the word 'sex' without blushing.

Another revolutionary, Jesus Christ, for example, outraged the culture of his time to such an extent they (society, the community, the mob, people en masse, whatever you want to call people formed in a group) strung him up and crucified him. 'Crucify him! Crucify him!' they roared. His friends disappeared into the crowd. It took years of individual struggle before he too became part of the group, the culture of the Western world.

To illustrate the relationship between culture and language, let us consider the way words change in meaning over generations. An obvious example is the word 'gay'. Originally it meant 'merry'. Then the homosexual community commandeered the word for their own purposes to advertise the fact that homosexuals might lack respectability in society but nevertheless, they were fun. And then school children of all people resisted this enlightenment and gave the word an extra twist so that it also came to mean 'lame' which word, in turn, has been given a secondary meaning. So culture evolves at the behest of society.

What old people have got is time. That is the golden ingredient of age. In the whiz, bang, wallop of a working day where one is forever clamouring for a piece of the action there is precious little opportunity to play the game of life. Your conscious mind is being gobbled up by the job at hand and at the end of the day you are too tired, except to go the route of TV, nosh and bed. The average Scot spends just 47.5 minutes a day interacting outside work, reported the Office of National Statistics in February, 2003. He spends eight minutes a day helping others and four minutes in volunteer work. The rest of the time is spend doing telly and food and what is called 'household activities'. (Perhaps that means sex.)

The Games People Play, Thank Goodness

Culture can finally afford to take centre stage in retirement. What that means is you can see which mind games are being played in any society you choose to join or happen to find yourself in, and become an expert practitioner. You too can become a socialite. Please get rid of the idea that this is a derogatory term: as Professor Robert Winston wrote in his book: *The Human Mind,* 'Social interaction is one of the most taxing parts of human existence.'

Look at the style of friend and neighbour, the lovely Leonie Gibbs, and tell me she is wasting her time. In our tiny little toff world in our corner of the globe she is a cultural icon because on top of great personal style, she can also wield a paint brush and handle a sculptor's chisel. I call her Leonie da Vinci. To get a flavour of her and to enjoy the play of her, I will give you an extract of a dinner party at her house that I ferreted away in my diary. I am not saying she is old because I would have to be executed but even she would have to admit to a little seasoning:

'Hilarious dinner at Phoeneas. Leonie on killing form. Couple of great quotes: 'I'm a great believer in not taking decisions. Decisions only lead to things happening and then anything can happen' and, 'By our age, peoples' lives are so complicated they can gobble you up and I'm not to be gobbled.'

She gave a spirited defence of the literary qualities of *Fifty Shades of Grey.* She noticed a lot of innuendo and use of words used for sex being applied in other contexts like using the word 'up', 'thrust' and 'cock' for example, in a passage about field sports. 'He cocked the gun and thrust his hands in his pockets and came up with a couple of 12 bore cartridges', she improvised, milking the key words.

Also talked rather well about the shape of the story and its rhythm, how the mundane and procedural stuff emphasised by contrast the shock of the explicitly erotic passages that would crop up every so often.

We agreed that women had gone crazy for the book because it had finally made literary porn respectable for them and women were never going to do anything sexual unless it was first made respectable. It's stylish but acceptable, and its very faintly suggestive cover was the secret of its success at the bookstands.

Inevitably, we got on to the subject of spanking. Most of the women demurred but Shenka said it depended who was doing the spanking – as long as the guy was rich and handsome.

'So you would take a slap or two from Henry Keswick?'

'Only if he lost weight!'

There probably has not been a dinner party in the country that has not discussed that book but I thought Leonie and Shenka did quite a good job. They certainly gave us a laugh.

Inspired by the girls, I had a rare moment of whimsy myself. 'What do you think of that?' I said to Georgie Rutherford, indicating my dessert – a custard tart full to the brim with cream, not a drop spilt.

'How are you going to eat it?'

'I'll think of a way.'

You find great players in the most unlikely situations. I sponsored an undernourished child called Esther from Ghana on a paltry monthly direct debit. Plan, the plainly named charity, sent me literature describing the lives of my sponsored kid's family. Life was physically tough and without distraction. A lot of their day was spent in search of wood and the carrying of water. Cooking was done over an open fire.

The charity's appeal letter went on to say: 'Esther's family, like their friends and neighbours, has a very small income and it is a struggle to be able to meet their basic needs. However, the families in the Aworworso Kpeti community have a rich social life.' That is what a lot of people do not appreciate about the Third World. Very often their social life is a lot better than ours. They go in for communal living and to that extent their culture is richer.

Obviously hardly anybody, as such, had a full time paid job in the community so they had acres of time to interact with one another. Sounds like a golden old age, except that is their lives.

A few years later, fired up by Bob Geldof's 'Make Poverty History' campaign, I created a charity of my own called Twinaid. The idea was to twin a UK town with an African town and we could trade financial aid for spiritual renewal. In my hometown of Inverness, the council had just agreed to spend £6 million on some unnecessary pavement widening scheme and a little bit of pedestrianisation in the town centre near my pub. My master plan was to embarrass the town councillors into re-allocating that money.

Apparently a tenner keeps an African alive for a week. Shit, I thought, £6 million could buy you half a dozen tribes. And I thought the sacrifice wouldn't be too great because I don't want to be seriously inconvenienced, but we could just manage the narrower pavements we had been happily walking on for the last 100 years and hell, I know it's crazily daring of me, but I will even risk walking across non-pedestrianised roads.

So I flew out with a couple of friends, Chris Swift and Bastie Rous. to Kenya to find a suitable town to twin and to research my project. They had both worked out in colonial Africa in earlier days and they said Kenya was the nicest country in the continent with the best climate and properly run could be a very prosperous country. It had plenty of potential.

They would help introduce me to relevant people and show me round the place. I wanted to take some heart-rending photographs of starving Kenyans and hear some amazing uplifting stories of human endurance which I could then knock up into an appeal leaflet with which I could raise money back home.

Photographically speaking, I was most disappointed not to find one starving person. I was really looking for a pot belly. That is what is so frustrating about hunger. For the most part you can't see it. I assume it is there but maybe it is not or maybe it just flares up in times of drought. At least there was a lot of astonishing poverty. So I could help there. Maybe use funds to set up a little business through a third party.

There was another thing that surprised me about my visit. Chris and Bastie took me round to see their various friends all over Kenya and we did dinner, bed and breakfast in one fabulous oasis of wealth after another: wide-spreading houses with the most beautiful lush gardens and hot and cold running black servants who stepped aside as you walked past them. The white guys were not racist ogres, as I was expecting. They were thoroughly enterprising and very hospitable. But one thing they did not have for all their privilege was the amazing social life of the black folk in their towns and villages.

We eventually settled on the town of Nanyuki to twin with Inverness. I thanked Chris and Bastlie for their whistle-stop tour of life as it used to be in the days of *White Mischief* but I had not come to Kenya to be pampered. I wanted to get to grips with life in the raw. I was on a mission. Chris and Bastie said they loved to help but there was still a couple of addresses needed checking out and within a trice one was helicoptered to one place and the other was chauffeured to another.

So I walked into the town of Nanyuki by myself. Within 100 yards I had picked up a guide, a guy who said he was a photographer but I could see no evidence of any demand for his services even if he really did have a camera. However his house was a breeze block two room affair with a television and so he was obviously comparatively well off.

What amazed me was that he knew everybody in the town. Literally, it took at least three hours to cross town because of the number of people who stopped and chatted with him. It was just a sequence of laughing and teasing and jokes. Happiness, not quiet contentment, but a real buoyancy of spirit, was what I was treated to witnessing during my weekend with Michael, my snapper friend.

At six o'clock he told me to go back to the club, the white compound, because no white man stayed out in town after dark. I said surely I was safe with him by my side and anyway I was a publican. I wanted to see what the Nanyuki nightlife was like. So he invited me back to his house for supper and his wife knocked us up what looked like a huge lump of mashed potato with specks of tomato and onion and maybe even morsels of meat. I don't know about its nourishment value but I can vouch that I have hardly ever felt so full in all my life. I felt as bloated as if I had just had Christmas lunch.

His ten year-old daughter sat by my side stroking my arm astonished by its smoothness. We then went on a pub crawl of the three pubs in the town and some very beautiful tall black girls found me irresistible. Never has my sex appeal proven so devastating. I only had to walk into a bar and the most beautiful women gradually stopped what they were doing and started circling me. Michael had to spoil it all and tell me they were after my money.

'O prostitutes, you mean!' I exclaimed.

'I wouldn't use that word,' he laughed. 'Not out loud. It's not polite.'

Next day we went to church. It was packed and I was the only white guy there. What a joyous occasion! How different to our boring and sparse little services back home. They were singing and chanting and praying at full pelt: homilies and proverbs and shouts of praise and people swaying in unison. It went on for a long time and I was happily dozing off in my seat allowing the experience to flood my senses when suddenly I discovered everybody was looking at me and Michael gave me a nudge in the ribs. I was expected to get up and say something.

So I went all Churchillian, as I do if I have to say something in public without warning. It buys you time. It means you don't rush your words and the great man's tone helps you rattle off big sounding phrases which mean nothing. 'I bring you greetings from the North. I come from a country far away where it snows. I extend the hand of friendship across the waters and thank you for your gracious welcome,' I said and then, for no apparent reason, I added the words: 'in your midst'.

Well, they had me up on the altar in no time along with two

other favoured members of the congregation, all of whom were holding farmyard animals of one sort or another and somebody planted a cockerel in my arms.

Afterwards, in the foyer of the church, I was introduced to a young boy who apparently had scored the seventh highest marks in his A-levels in the whole of Kenya and he just needed financial help to pay for university and could I be of assistance. I gave vague promises and said I would think about it.

What a community! What a weekend! Such automatic affection extended to me, a perfect stranger. I know they were all after my money but I am quite used to that in the UK. At home in Inverness I am quite troutish in a little pond.

I went to Nanyuki thinking I could in some way relieve their misery and came away thinking they could help us with ours. You know the statistics. One in three people in London live alone. But we know perfectly well, we would never want to trade places because we far prefer pleasure to happiness. Wouldn't you prefer mild discontent on a full stomach than outrageous happiness on an empty one?

Culture is not Cool

Culture is the stuff that makes you laugh. Nations have different senses of humour because they have different cultures. You can see from their comedy films that Americans love slapstick and all things scatological with special reference to the bottom or 'ass' as they will have it, what we call a donkey. The Germans and the Japanese enjoy seeing other people in pain. We find embarrassment funny and, of course, we are famous for our irony.

Disconnected people, people without culture, are not amused. A surprising number of people do not genuinely laugh. Making laughing noises, showing your teeth and creasing your eyes does not necessarily mean you have got the joke or even if you have, that you find it remotely funny. Neuroscientists have identified 18 different types of smile but only one gives that warm feeling. It is called the Duchenne smile. It needs two sets of muscles, which can be moved at will and is controlled by the motor cortex, and another around the eyes called the norbicularis oculi, which responds only to genuine emotion. And it's controlled by the anterior cingulae region of the limbic system. I wonder if prayer stimulates the limbic system. Whether it does or it doesn't, part of my daily prayer routine includes the following appeal: 'Please God, may Thy Sacred Hands massage the anterior cingulae of my limbic system so that life puts a smile on my face and not one of the seventeen fake ones but a proper little Duchenne'

That is not a joke. I pray for real appreciation. I pray to be genuinely amused. I call it 'grace'. I know, from watching other people, that it is only people who are profoundly connected to their culture who laugh and smile like a Duchenne. So really what I am doing is praying for connection.

Amy, the beautiful female lead, who is a perfectionist, in the 2013 global bestseller *Gone Girl*, is a certain type of modern, highly educated woman brought up on film and television like the rest of us and for whom life is permanent role play. She says of herself, and I wonder if this is not also the author, Gillian Flynn, talking: 'Nick (her husband) loved a girl who doesn't exist. I was pretending, the way I often did, pretending to have a personality. I can't help it, it's what I have always done: The way some women change fashion regularly, I change personalities. What persona feels good, what's coveted, what's au courant? I think most people do this, they just don't admit it.'

'Cool Girl' is her favourite persona for attracting men. 'Cool girl' is fit and funny and sexy: every young man's pin up. Anybody who claims to enjoy giving oral sex is faking it. They are playing 'Cool Girl', claims the heroine/author. Who wants to swallow raw egg white in their right minds? The problem Amy found was that she could not maintain 'Cool Girl' after the initial stages of her marriage.

'She's not the girl I thought I was dating.' comments her husband, Nick ruefully. 'She can quote funny things, but she doesn't actually like funny things. She'd rather not laugh, anyway. In fact she'd rather than I did not laugh either or be funny, which is awkward since it's my job, but to her, it's all a waste of time.'

I would describe her as somebody disconnected from her culture, alienated from the group. I see her as a casualty of her upbringing. She was an only child, doted on by her parents both of whom were psychologists and so doubly focused. She was made to feel unique rather than part of a family of siblings.

Amy remembers in her childhood 'always being baffled by other children. I would be at a birthday party and watch the other kids giggling and making faces, and I would try to do that, too, but I wouldn't understand why. I would sit there with the tight elastic thread of the birthday hat parting the pudge of my under chin, with the grainy frosting of the cake bluing my teeth, and I would try to figure out why it was fun.'

Sometimes you get a clash of two cultures where the same incident can be considered hilarious in one environment and tragic in another. I had a business called Large Holiday Houses which let mansions in Scotland for week-long holiday lets. Our main competitor was a company called CKD who had created a website called Large Holiday Homes in order to syphon off some of our trade. My partner, Wynne Holmes, in LHH was particularly miffed by this little business spoiler tactic and wondered how we could get our own back at CKD.

It so happened that one of the partners of CKD was a country neighbour of mine called John Robin Bound. His nickname was JR. That weekend we had both been invited to a shoot by Chris Swift, the guy who had accompanied me to Kenya. I am a very reluctant shot for no other reason that I can never hit anything. The day progressed along its inevitable course with me knee-deep in empty cartridge shells and pheasants taking the piss out of me when one particular pheasant made its way up a valley. I was on one side of the valley and JR was on the other. Well, I missed the pheasant and got JR. A pellet clipped his ear and he shot up like a scalded cat.

I apologised profusely and he quite rightly tore a strip off me and I was evicted from the shoot in disgrace without lunch, or rather I offered to leave there and then and nobody demurred. My host, Chris Swift, escorted me to my car and very kindly said the incident would go no further than the shoot but by the end of the weekend, the hushed question on everybody's lips in our wider social circle was inevitably: 'Who shot JR?' When I told Wynne Holmes what had happened, I couldn't stop her laughing.

For culture to exist, you have got to care. What they care most about in business is success and that means beating, if not actually eliminating, your competitors. The sheer joy when a rival goes bust is one of the deepest pleasures of commerce. Safety is the prime prerequisite of field sports. Obviously people at a shoot care more about not hitting one another than killing birds and animals. So no wonder what was funny in the office was very serious at the pheasant shoot at the time.

By that reckoning, the less we care, the less the culture, and we increasingly live in an indifferent age where most experience is vicarious. 'What happens to emotional development as the ratio of vicarious experience to real experience rises?' writes Alvin Toffler in *Future Shock.* 'No previous generation has been exposed to one tenth the amount of vicarious experiences that we lavish on ourselves and our children today and no one anywhere has any real idea about the impact of this monumental shift on personality.' He was writing in the Sixties. We know now . . . a mushrooming of the fake . . . a ballooning of the phony.

A professor of psychology, Joyce Catlett, author of *Fear of Intimacy,* writes 'Spending hours in front of the screen cuts people of from their feelings.' So they fake them instead. Just look at Lady Di's funeral when literally hundreds of thousands of our fellow countrymen indulged in an orgy of sentimentality about the woman. None of these people who lined the streets of London publicly weeping and wailing in mourning on the day of her funeral even knew her and infinitesimally few of them had even exchanged a single remark with her. It was not like she was Churchill. Lady Di did not save the country, and that means you and me. We did not personally owe her a debt of gratitude. In fact, she had died too late on the Saturday night for *The Sunday Times* to pull their open-spread, double-page hatchet job of her. They attacked her for behaving like Euro trash with vacuous playboys. She was careering out of control and proving to be a deep embarrassment for the royal family, they wrote. My God, did *The Sunday Times* change their tune the following Sunday!

In our defence we can claim that we are too exhausted to care. Every work place is overworked and understaffed because the economy is unbalanced. We have reverted to Victorian times where the rich get richer on the back of not just the poor but the rest of us as well.

We all suffer from sensory overload. We are bombarded with a million mini decisions a day. The mobile phone will not leave us alone. We are being entertained to death in our switch, press and click age. Some people even dream about movie stars rather than real people. That is dreaming about dreaming. Even film about starving people in Africa comes with its own soundtrack.

And no other people in the world are subjected to as much cheap cultural product through mechanised medium as the Brits and Americans, although at least we have the ballast of the past. No wonder our culture is thinning to the point where we are beginning not to know who we are, which explains why everybody is posing. Look at Facebook.

We are stymied with self-consciousness. No wonder we drink and drug and shag to forget ourselves if only for the duration. No wonder we are amazed by how civilised are our Mediterranean counterparts by comparison when we come across them on our annual foreign holiday. I don't see, come the holiday season, drunken gangs of Spaniards shagging and fighting their way through the streets of Oxford or Edinburgh on a Saturday night.

The great thing about old age is you can stop the clock. You can regain control of your life. You have just stepped off the merry-go-round. You do not need to dance to anybody else's tune. You have known the facts of life, the real ones not the silly sex ones, for decades and now's the time to implement those hundred resolutions about how life should be lived if only you had the time and opportunity. You can so deepen yourself in old age. There is no reason you cannot become as cultured as a Frenchman. There is no excuse at all why you should not now finally become the person you were born to be. Memo to self: I am going to learn one new poem a month so that I know it as well as a Catholic knows the Rosary. Second memo: I am going to concentrate on somebody until I care about them. Stalk the little bastard. Imagine you are a private detective of the mind. If you can care about one unrelated person, you can care about anyone. That is power.

At Least you Finally Know how to Behave

Moral relativism and the cult of the individual have made little gods of us all. No wonder so many of us are all at sea, not waving but drowning, although you have finally probably worked a lot of it out by a process of trial and error by the time you have reached old age.

Where the past no longer exists and every teenager thinks they know best, and we all genuflect before the altar of youth and beauty because it looks so good and moves so well on film and Prime Ministers are squirts barely out of their thirties, and only the moment matters – you lose perspective. If you really want to know what it is like to have your society run by the young, I refer you to the chaos of the Middle Ages where everybody died by the age of forty. How can we ever learn anything if we never listen to the old? Wisdom only comes with age. You simply can't fast forward it.

Alternatively, if culture is the generational roll-over of accumulated wisdom seamlessly interwoven into the texture of our language and reflected in our attitudes handed down to us by our parents, it must be important that we at least listen to them even if we dismiss our grandparents as doddery old fools. It is only now at the age of 58 that I have finally started listening to my mother. I was too busy and distracted before and anyway, was doing all the talking myself. I am twenty-five years too late for my father. What a treasure trove of musings and memories he took to the grave with him and it would only have taken the simple device of asking questions and bending an attentive ear!

The problem is that the television is far more influential than the parent, let alone the grandparent, and television, for all its sophistry, is adolescent. It is all about cool and attitude and sound bites and action and jokes and argument and emotion and sex and violence and cars and fame and food and luxuries, so that no one is bored for a moment.

Without culture no one knows how to behave any more. You have got to learn everything from scratch. You have got to work it all out for yourself, playing a life-long game of hunt the thimble with the truth and thinking, analysing, watching, listening and reading just to work out how to behave and hopefully you get there before you die. The start of old age is obviously the last opportunity.

The problem about moral relativism is that it puts you in charge of proceedings. It is like making a criminal both judge and jury of his own case. You won't be surprised to hear about the very high rate of acquittals. Nobody wants to feel bad and if you can deceive yourself into thinking that what you have just gone and done is not actually bad, well it's only human. Yippee, sin no longer exists!

I will give you a story about relative morality that had amazing consequences at the end of a long night in Liberated London when I was in hot pursuit of a beautiful, dark haired woman with my usual total disregard for personal psychic safety, my ego bracing itself for rejection and my brain desperately seeking inspiration. She had what I call peasant good looks – rather heavy-featured and she scraped in under five foot-five, which is normally my cut-off point with a woman. I'm a bit size-ist that way. She was a little spacious below decks. Her legs were built for rough terrain. She was generous in her figure. Almost extravagant with her bottom which you dearly wanted to pat, which was strange because her name was Patsy. What lit up the entire package was a seraphic smile. She had full lips and a lovely set of straight white teeth which made me want to amuse her as much as possible.

I don't need to go to great lengths about her but suffice it to say that she was a nurse for the handicapped. Middle age had put paid to a teenage marriage to a budding pop star whose promise had not led to any recording contracts. Sexually speaking, she free-lanced for a while before embarking on a couple of lengthy relationships and now here she was at the age of forty, mildly attached. I felt there was room for manoeuvre and last night was my window of opportunity when I took her out to dinner and I must admit, although I say it myself, I thought I played my cards rather well considering I had been out of the game for so long and let's face it, I was not looking at a row of court cards in my hand. I led with some gentle enquiries, picked up a few easy tricks with some tried and tested stories, finessed her with deep interest in whatever gibberish she was talking about and then trumped her with some nifty little ruminations of my own.

There were two things I liked about her. She had a tremendous caring nature. I care about handicapped people in principle but looking after them would bore me to tears. She actually enjoyed her job. She loved her wheelchair cases. She even went to bed with one. The other thing was the delight she took in small accomplishments. She had just moved into rented accommodation and she was full of the little improvements she was going to make.

Also, there was no nonsense about her. She liked to be surprised by the truth. Mind you, her truths were very different to mine. She was a typical modern girl. God did not exist and morality was a moveable feast. She did not see anything wrong with prostitution. She said it was infinitely preferable to working at the checkout in Tesco's.

'I am a care worker. I could be a sex worker. Both professions offer comfort to people in need. The only difference is the pay.'

'Forget about the issues of morality,' I replied. 'What about the psychological damage?'

'None. I know. I've done it.'

Flummoxed, I think is the word, I was.

'After the break-up of my marriage, I did it, by way of contrast. I just wanted to know what it felt like. And I tell you, I felt genuinely empowered. You were in total control, not the other way about as usual. You held the whip hand, so to speak!'

I spluttered over my espresso.

'Let me tell you,' she continued. 'It was sexy and extremely addictive. I only did it once, as I say, just to see what it was like and to prove a point to myself, to show I really was free. I was free to do what I want, irrespective of convention. And I wanted to do it again but I decided not to go down that route. I phoned up a friend of mine whom I quite liked the look of. He had been single for quite a while not having sex and I thought I could do him a favour. I know he fancied me. He accepted my offer which was £200 for half an hour. Actually, it took two hours and he gave me £800. I've never told anybody that and I don't know why I have told you – probably to shock you out of your smug Christian piety. What do you think of me now, eh?'

As you might have picked up, I was absolutely at a loss to say anything and a silence fell between us and then I suddenly emptied my pockets to produce a £20 note and I said: 'Would £20 buy me a kiss?'

The New Old

It is the work of a moment for the ingenious mind of man to change the goal posts and let's face it, immorality is the ultimate own goal because the human psyche is not designed to prosper on vice. My father only gave me one piece of advice in his whole life and that was never to justify bad behaviour. 'You are going to get things wrong in life but please don't kid yourself that they are alright,' he said. He had seen too many people make that fundamental mistake in their lives. It is not the immoral act that causes irretrievable damage, it is the lies you tell yourself to justify the immorality that makes the journey back to virtue impossible. You get lost in the labyrinth of lies you have told yourself.

Guilt is good. It shows you are not a self-liar. I have seen the alternative on television. It was the repeat of a programme made after the fall of the Berlin Wall and the release of information held by the East German secret police, the Stasi. This programme reported that 80 to 90 per cent of arrests of Jews in Nazi Germany came about as a result of ordinary Germans informing the Gestapo. The TV reporter confronted one of the informants who had denounced her neighbour resulting in the person's arrest and disappearance.

The attitude of the woman then in her early sixties was astonishing. She agreed that the document of denunciation was hers and the signature was hers. She said she had forgotten all about it, as if her betrayal was a minor misdemeanour. She laughed in a superior fashion at the TV investigator, humouring him that he should make such an issue of it. She said by way of mitigation that she had never joined the Nazi youth. Eventually she was so exasperated at the reporter's attitude that she said: 'I mean really, you're still bringing it up 50, 51 years later!' Eventually she said: 'Oh look it's raining.' The interview had taken place on a park bench.

We are the first generation of the new old. We are the first modern pensioners and we know how people younger than us feel. We were brought up by telly too. There is none of this incomprehension our predecessors suffered from. We understand the confusion of the young and why they buy blitheringly obvious self-help books by the truck load. We are in a position to let them benefit from our life long struggle with freedom. No other generation before us could do what they wanted and we have paid the price. We know the importance of codes of conduct worked out by the great religions of this Earth and how paltry is our little pipsqueak brains compared to the cumulative might of the great minds of the past.

We have lived through revolutionary times where the old order was completely turned on its head. We have seen what has happened to ourselves and to others and so we have learnt respect. We are now finally in a position to pass that attitude on to the people coming up behind us so that they don't waste as much time as we have trying to learn how to live, instead of just enjoying it.

It is why I have written this book.

CHAPTER NINE

When your Knees Give Way

I was thinking about a response from a friend of mine called Rachel Humphries to a biblical reference I had made in the course of a discussion about how to milk a millionaire. I said we could get a millionaire to contribute to a charity we were thinking of setting up by appealing to his natural feelings of fear of the afterlife. I said we could drop the words 'camel', 'needle' and 'pyramid' into the conversation and then quote the line in the bible that goes 'Charity covereth a multitude of sins'. And then we would triumphantly conclude our sales pitch with the words: 'So you see, all you have to do is give us some money and then you can carry on living it up with a clear conscience!'

Rachel said the words 'sin' and 'afterlife' were actually meaningless to her and she had never even heard about it being as difficult for a camel to go through the eye of the needle as a rich man to go to heaven. She had been brought up in an atheist household.

'How did you celebrate Christmas then?'

'We were told about Santa Claus.'

I said it was amazing that she was told an outright lie rather than something that could be true. Rachel said she did not need any of these fantasy figures to enjoy her life. I looked at her and thought what a well-balanced, socially integrated, highly articulate, thoroughly good and well intentioned, basically happy young woman she was. She is well connected within herself and other people. She was brought up in the bosom of a family in the heart of her culture, within the boundaries of her community. She gets her sense of well-being from a good communion with other people. She's got all the

126

people she needs and anybody who meets her quickly loves her. She's got such a lovely personality, and she's not bad looking.

And I thought that's all well and good during the light hearted years of youth, but as life goes on it gets more serious, until by late middle age you realise that basically you are on your own, although family and friends can dilute the solitude. They can offer comfort. They cannot solve the problem. Gabriel Garcia Màrquez wrote one of the most famous books in the world: *One Hundred Years of Solitude.* He meant life.

What happens when things go wrong and you are attacked by illness, or ambushed by tragedy, or the Wheel of Fortune starts to roll away from you? How do you cope with what I call the triple curse of life: LSD – Loneliness, Sickness and Depression?

So many and so much of our lives are spent trying to overcome or prevent these three scourges. Because we have broken up community, loneliness has become the black hole of modern society into which millions of people disappear, especially the old. It is not flagged up either by health professionals or politicians because there is no way of providing statistics for such an abstract notion, although in 2013, the *Evening Standard* boldly claimed that one in four Londoners consciously felt lonely for a part of every single day.

Depression is much easier to quantify, just count the pills. We have been consuming five times as many anti-depressants as 30 years ago. Thomas Hardy spotted the start of all our mental problems when he was looking back to the time just before the industrial revolution really got under way and he wrote of Angel Clare: 'Considering his position he became wonderfully free from the chronic melancholy which is taking hold of the civilised races with the decline of belief in a beneficent Power.'

Sickness levels have got a lot worse because paradoxically our health care has got so much better, now that we live way past our natural allotted time span of three score and ten. Whereas in the good old days, one serious heart attack or one decent stroke or just a brush with cancer would provide you with a one-way ticket to 'ride the midnight train to Slab City', as Moe the barman from *The Simpsons* so delightfully put it – now you are kept tortuously alive to live to die another day.

Thomas Merton, a great American monk, wrote:

When a man suffers, he is most alone. Therefore, it is in suffering that we are most tested as persons. How can we face the awful interior questioning? What shall we answer when we come to be examined by pain? Without God, we are no longer persons. We lose our manhood and our dignity. We become dumb animals under pain, happy if we can behave at least like quiet animals and die without too much commotion.

What do you do if you are depressed? What do you do if you are lonely? Madly rush around seeking the company of other people, give yourself a series of treats, distract yourself with work, take some pills, pay a therapist, drink some alcohol, watch a lot of telly, check out some porn? What do you do if you are sick? Go to bed. Then what? Get lonely and depressed?

Prayer is an alternative although, on the face of it, it may well feel there and then like a terrible waste of time when you could be getting on with something useful. What we don't call a waste of time is a morning on the telephone or doing promotion on the Internet, attempting to persuade people to part with their money. We call that a good morning's work and we feel satisfied that we have employed our time profitably.

On the other hand, it seems profligate to spend valuable conscious time on your knees brainwashing yourself into goodness, dwelling on a legendary character's model life and his mother, asking for favours for yourself and your friends and relations off somebody who may well not exist, and almost certainly will not accede to your wishes, (although I admit petitionary prayer is not the primary reason you pray).

I would argue that it is a waste of your time not to say your morning prayers because it means for yet another day you have not taken the opportunity to get closer to God, yet another day which you have not dedicated to carrying out His wishes. Getting to heaven is much more important than making money.

'For a small living, men run a great way. For eternal life, many will scarce move a foot,' wrote Thomas à Kempis in the Middle Ages. No change there then.

Without preparation, life degenerates into slapstick. You become accident prone. Our family motto is 'Je suis prest' which does not mean: 'I am a priest.' It means 'I am ready.' I am prepared. In starting the day with a recommended dose of 20 minutes of prayer and 10 minutes of devotional reading, I am carrying out my family mantra. Who would not prepare for an important event and there is no more important event in your life than the day in front of you?

Successful prayer gives you grace, or to put it in secular terms, it makes you feel good about yourself. It puts you in a good mood. It is a flying start to the day. And if depression is your problem, it keeps it at bay. 'Pray and you will have the deepest joy, you will have peace, you will overcome your tiredness, you will also become handsome and beautiful,' said Our Lady to the six young people in the Balkans, whose experiences created the worldwide movement, the Medjugorje Visionaries. Unfortunately, Our Lady is not guaranteeing film-star looks. She is, of course, talking about inner beauty that shines through your face. Still, spiritual beauty ages better than physical beauty. Good news for us old crocks.

The Best Decision in my Life

I would say that the best decision of my life was not to give up religion, as all my schoolmates did, when I hit the ripe old age of fourteen and a half. My friends felt differently. Obviously they thought they had enough experience of the world and had read enough theology to be able to dismiss the idea of God for the rest of their days and concentrate their active thinking time instead on serious things like city careers and pop culture. And I am not joking. That is exactly what they thought at the time and it has been mostly what has happened ever since. I know hardly anybody who has taken up religion after having dropped it in their early teens – which argues their disbelief is intuitive rather than rational.

No, God always made a lot of sense to me. I was not put off by the fact that I could not see Him. I couldn't see electricity, but it still worked. And my teenage decision to stick by Him for life, which in practical terms meant praying to Him every day for up to four minutes, although as the years have gone by I have lengthened my stride to twenty minutes with a ten minute read (despite writing regularly to myself about the need to do a whole hour first thing in the morning but you know how it is – breakfast beckons).

But even that tiny daily investment has saved me from those Twin Devils of the Mind: loneliness and depression. Cursed by terrible shyness before the opposite sex, having been brought up with three brothers and sent to an all-male boarding school, my youth was to all intents and purposes celibate and now once again I return to that state having mislaid my wife. But those solitary years have not given me a day of loneliness.

And I have had hairy moments in my life, several brushes with bankruptcy and, of course, losing my wife to a friend, neighbour and cousin: incidentally, that's one person not three although, to be accurate, I suppose three people were involved in the entire marital breakdown. In fact, there was a sort of arithmetic progression because her first boyfriend was just a friend and the second one was a friend and a neighbour, and the third, and I suppose, what you might call the current owner occupier, pulled off a hat trick being a friend, a neighbour and a cousin. But you would be amazed to hear that despite this pretty comprehensive humiliation, it has never given me a day of depression.

Actually, a lot of the time, it made me quite adrenalised. That is how trauma took me and the times when it brought me low with a kind of dull lassitude – I would not call that depression. That was grief. Real depression comes out of nowhere for no apparent reason, robbing you of your energy and giving you an overwhelming nihilistic feeling of complete pointlessness.

Prayer is Cheaper than Prozac

Prayer defeats depression. What is being crushed by depression is your spirit, the very same spirit that is being nurtured by prayer. That is the point of prayer. It's to make you feel good deep inside you. Successful prayer gives you daily bounce. And as regards the banishment of loneliness, you're never alone with God. Actually, there's two ways to read that last solemn statement, but you know which way I mean it because, of course, God is the one person you are alone with when you are down on your knees in prayer.

My friend, Anna Wallace, suggested another reason for my good fortune in managing to avoid loneliness and depression. She put it down to the fact that I come from a loving and supportive family but I know a lot of people who are similarly blessed who still succumb to either or both of those Twin Devils.

I am not boasting about it. I am just reporting back to you my surprise. When Sarah left me, I fully expected to have to learn to live intermittently with LSD for the rest of my days until I found a replacement for her. We all know Sickness is waiting in the wings. I am just very pleasantly surprised and in scouring around looking for an explanation, I attribute my lucky escape to the fact that I have been on my knees for over half a century, starting at 3 or 4 minutes a day and working up to my current daily quotient of half-an-hour, plus one hour on Sunday at Church, and it has transpired not to have been a waste of time.

If you add up the time, I have probably prayed to God one way or another for a total of 3,000 hours because I have factored in a percentage of days which I missed out on. 3,000 hours is the amount of time they say it takes to master a foreign language, so I must now be fluent at prayer. Anyway, it is quite a lot of time and I must say I do expect some form of pay back for that investment. I hope it helps free me from my past, ease my present and guarantee my future.

The reason why the afterlife is so much more important than this life is because it lasts so much longer and, if what we are saying is prayer – communion with this possibly mythical figure called God – has such a beneficial effect on how you get through your allotted time on earth that it rids you of the debilitating effects of LSD, how much more important it is to adhere to the teachings of the Lord, if it is going to have a similarly beneficial effect on your time in eternity.

Hey, Peace Man!

Religion by itself no more makes you a good person than education or sport does. Study is an attempt to improve your mind. Exercise is an attempt to improve your body. Prayer is an attempt to improve your spirit. These hard earned improvements can be put to good use or not. Power can be abused. That is precisely what fundamentalists, fanatics and thugs do.

Feeling like a victim is a form of powerlessness. Self-pity, lack of resilience, lack of stamina, collapse of morale, loss of initiative, flat lining energy, feelings of pointlessness – these are all signs of a failure of spirit. What prayer does is nourish that spirit. Prayer can empower you even to defeat loneliness. You can put a man of prayer in jail and he will conquer that ghost. Jesus Christ did not feel like a victim even though he was made a scapegoat by his own people. Prayer enables meaning.

The art of life is to express the very fullness of your own unique spirit within the scope of your limited circumstances. What we so often find ourselves spending our lives doing is attempting to improve our circumstances rather than ourselves. The point of prayer is that it allows your spirit to grow within any environment.

Too much television depresses the spirit, as does too much drink and drugs. Actually, successful prayer is like a good stiff drink in that it raises your spirit wonderfully and afterwards there follows whatever you might call the feeling that is the opposite to a hangover. I don't think there is even a word for it. Might you call it a lift off or enlightenment perhaps?

The job of prayer is to reform our habit of thought, to ameliorate our consciousness, to increase our awareness. We need to break free of inherited attitudes that restrict our movement of mind. We need to overcome vices peculiar to class: the working class with its inclination towards ignorance and prejudice, the middle class with its timidity and its comforts, the upper class with its arrogance and its exclusivity, and the aristocracy's idleness and amorality.

We have all got circular minds and we must try and enlarge that rotary motion to include our neighbour with all his concerns. An addict is a man caught in an ever diminishing vicious cycle of repetitive thought. A man of prayer eschews all forms of obsession. He is full of play. His mind revolves like a globe, open to all manner of people.

We need prayer if we don't want to take tranquillisers. Prayer gives peace. Is peace important? Of course, we want to banish feelings of nervousness, anxiety and tension – what we all to a lesser or greater extent suffer from in the general harassment of modern life. Why do you think people smoke cigarettes? Why do they smoke dope?

There is a brief moment of seriousness in a very witty rom-com called *Rumour Has It* where the Kevin Costner character, who is a ridiculously charming and handsome dotcom millionaire, extraordinarily mentions the word 'peace' to the absurdly charming and beautiful Jennifer Aniston, within the context of talking about the three days he had spent on a romantic idyll with the Aniston character's mother. Incidentally, the Costner character is a generation older than the Aniston character but the age gap can be bridged by his pulling power and it's the work of five minutes of film before he is bedding the daughter as well. The Costner character has everything the world can offer and yet he very revealingly says: 'Those were the happiest three days of my life. The only time I felt peaceful.'

Not that I am one to crow. I have a face like Prince Charles's. I always look mildly anxious, which is not surprising considering I have lived my adult life a phone call away from bankruptcy: the lot of a small town entrepreneur. I can't tell you the number of people I have never met before who are moved to utter this little modern quip: 'It might never happen.'

'How do you know?' I reply.

Occasionally, as if by accident, we are visited by a feeling of a light calm and we think: 'How nice! That is how I should be feeling all the time.' It is as if everything falls into place and life suddenly becomes easy and we take casual enjoyment in just anybody we happen to come across. Women in the aftermath of childbirth feel like that. Physical exercise can have the same short term effect. Prayer is an attempt to make that feeling permanent.

I was briefly converted to a spiritual life immediately after I came back from my pilgrimage to Medjugorje in the Balkans, when I attempted to follow Our Lady's advice to the letter although I could not really manage her instructions about the need to fast. This was what I wrote in my diary in the first flush of my enthusiasm before I reverted to normalcy:

I have got the secret of happiness. But before I tell you, first you have to ask yourself, what is happiness? It is a feeling. It is a feeling of lightness, ease and fullness. It makes you look forward to seeing people. It makes you enjoy doing what is immediately in front of you. It is a wonderful aid to concentration. It gets you out of yourself and into somebody or something else. What is the secret of happiness? How do you get it? Simple. Get up at 6, wash your teeth and shave if you have to and then pray till 8 without having breakfast. Not so much as a sip of coffee shall pass your lips. God will give you grace to last you one day and a tiny bit over to put in the bank.

How to Become a Saint in a Week

You can become a saint in a week. Just follow Our Lady's instructions as relayed to the visionaries, and they are very tough. Pray three hours a day and fast on Wednesdays and Fridays. Every single Olympic athlete does the equivalent in terms of physical endurance every week of his sporting life. If the reward is great enough, you will put yourself through a lot. There is an argument to suggest that guarantee of personal salvation in the next world and the conquest of happiness in this world is an even greater prize than an Olympic medal.

You think I am exaggerating. You don't think you can become a saint in a week. The great medieval mystic, Master Eckhart, said that if there was such a thing as a spiritual journey, it would be a quarter of an inch long though many miles deep. So forget time. You are there, the moment you have the right attitude.

In the prologue to the *Benedictine Book of Prayer*, however, it is written:

Some may think the point of prayer is to get our own way with extraterrestrial help, or to save us from facing the problems of life, or to provide an escape from 'reality', or to give an emotional uplift that makes you feel good. Some may think that prayer is a way of expanding our consciousness which is achieved by our own self-discipline and personal effort at self-improvement. These are caricatures of what Christian prayer really is. There may be a strand of truth in some of them, but they miss the real point of prayer.

Alright, I have listed some of the caricatures – the beneficial side effects of prayer. The prologue then goes on to tell us the main point of prayer. It says it is not really about you at all. It is about God. Essentially prayer is not like aerobics. It is not a relaxation technique. Prayer, as an activity in itself, is no more important than a telephone. What is important is who is on the other end of the line. God gives us what the author of the prologue calls: 'love beyond imagining'. 'That is what prayer is about.' he writes.

Mother Teresa was once asked what she did in prayer.

'I listen to God.'

'What does he do?'

'He listens to me.'

Father Tomislav and Father Slkavko Barbaric, the two Franciscan monks supervising the Medjugorje Visionaries Experience, say: 'Prayer is a dialogue with God, speaking to God, without any special method of concentration.' So you can forget yoga as well.

One of the fruits of prayer is all the lateral ideas that pop into your head while you are concentrating on your devotions. Some people call the things that occur to you unbidden when you pray, as the workings of your subconscious, or the tiny voice of your Second Self, or communications from the Lord — all just different ways of saying that God is replying from the other end of the telephone because God is within you as well as without.

I was talking to my twenty something-year-old daughter, Vita, the other night, who like most modern youth does not spare God or any of His religions a thought. I said that as the years go by people either become more selfish or less so. No one stays the same because we are organic. Only religious people can become funda-mentally unselfish, I claimed, because the basic principle of religion, Christianity especially, *is* the other person, whereas the secular world is all about yourself and your rights.

Without God, you are an animal. Beneath the social veneer which is just our way of negotiating with one another, you will behave like an animal. You have no choice because you are one. That is the behaviourist argument. Being nice to somebody else is just a way of getting them to be nice to you.

A spiritual person, on the other hand, does not think he is an animal at all. He thinks he is 'a little lower than an angel' and so he tries to behave like one. An active religious man sets aside time each day in prayer to remind himself not to be selfish but to think of others, even at the cost of his own personal convenience. Furthermore, he goes to church on Sunday to be lectured to by a priest on this very subject and be given grace in the form of Holy Communion to carry out instructions.

Vita made the interesting point that, God or no God, normally selfish people can behave surprisingly unselfishly if their imagination was caught. I said that prayer is just an exercise of imagination.

Not to believe in God betrays a lack of imagination. The reason why some people cannot fall in love is because they lack poetic imagination. There's a great bit in my favourite book of all time, *The Horse's Mouth* by Joyce Carey, which sums up courtship in a paragraph:

Girl going past clinging to a young man's arm. Putting up her face like a duck to the moon. Drinking joy. Green in her eyes. Spinal curvature. No chin, mouth like a frog. Young man like a pug. Gazing down at his sweetie with the face of a saint reading the works of God. Hold on, maiden, you've got him. He's your boy. Look out, Puggy, that isn't a maiden you see before you, it's a work of imagination. Nail him, girlie. Nail him to the contract. Fly laddie, fly off with your darling vision before she turns into a frau, who spends her life thinking of what the neighbours think.

Why have imagination if you don't use it? Imagination is one of our three primary mental functions along with will and intellect. We need to exercise all three capabilities to sustain a growing relationship with God. We need to use our intellect to prove through reason the high probability of His very existence, our imagination to become aware of the presence of the Lord in prayer and our will to give us the self-discipline to develop spiritually throughout a life of distraction, disturbance and disappointment.

There is a huge literature about the philosophy of prayer but nothing much about how to pray, and I am as guilty as the next person. I have gassed on at length about its benefits but what have I got to say about how on earth you do it. Well, all I can do is to tell you what I do, what works for me.

The first thing I do is get my egg timer and set it for half an hour. Then I crack open a devotional book, read three pages and then with a biro underline meaningful lines. I choose three books and spend three years reading them three times each. I am currently reading: *Anam Cara* by John O'Donohue, *No Man Is An Island* by Thomas Merton and *Seeking God* by Basil Hume – the last two are written by monks for monks, but they are just as applicable for us lay folk. This is the opposite to speed reading. I read to incorporate these books into my mind so that they become a part of me. In the pages, I find a line that impresses me, learn it by heart and use it as a basis for my prayers that morning.

Then I make a declaration of faith to deal with my rational mind. As an aide-memoire I make a sign of the cross: 'In the name of the Father, the Son, the Holy Ghost, Amen.' Which I silently translate as: 'In the name of Order/Beauty, Love, Sanctity, Infinity, Morality: my instant five-point personal proof of the existence of God.

When my hand goes to my forehead – my brain and just below, my eyes – I think of Order/Beauty, which reminds me that where there is Order, there is an Architect, and the Earth is the last word in Order. It is also amazing in its sheer myriad beauty. Surely the work of divine genius: Leonardo Da Vinci times infinity.

Then my hand goes to my belly where all my feelings come from and I think of the love of Jesus Christ and I also think of roughly where in His anatomy he was speared while stretched out on the cross, reminding me of how he suffered for the love of us. I think of how a man of such wisdom and integrity and above all, love, could possibly have based his whole life on a lie: his claim that he was the Son of God. This guy did not arrive out of the blue. He was the Messiah. That was the whole point of the Old Testament. That was the big prophesy. That's why we had prophets.

Then my hand goes from shoulder to shoulder saying 'Holy Ghost'. The word 'Holy' makes me think of holy people who have devoted their lives to God and give off this extraordinary powerful vibe that is other worldly. The word 'Ghost' makes me think of Mystery: the mysterious circumstances of life – the fact that there never was a first moment because there was always one before it and the statistical impossibility of the very existence of Earth because of all the particular physical conditions that have got to be inch and degree perfect.

My hands finally come together in the middle of my body as I say Amen and I think of the core of my being, my soul: the seat of my conscience, the arbiter of my personal morality. If there was no God, we would not have a sense of right and wrong because we would just be animals.

Now I turn to the female half of my mind, my intuition, my imagination, my subconscious, my Second Self. I drop to my knees beside my bed, which is just the right height for my elbows. I say five decades of the rosary: Joyful for Monday and Thursday, Sorrowful for Tuesday and Friday and Triumphant for Wednesday and Saturday. I go to Church on Sunday.

The effect of saying the rosary is to occupy the surface of your mind and allow you to descend into your Second Self where real prayer can take place. I now imagine God is present in the room and Our Lady. I think it takes a minimum of five minutes to contact God. Our Lady is a little quicker because she is easier to imagine. Also, I am greatly helped by a photograph of the six Medjugorje visionaries' upturned faces seeing Herself, as they say in the Highlands.

Once I have got hold of both Our Lord and Our Lady in my imagination, I make two little home-made prayers to them. One to God:

> Park a blessing on my nut.
> And I will do Thy holy will.

And one to Our Lady:

> Kiss me, O Mother of Mine,
> And fill my heart full of love.

I think what is important is that you should remind yourself of your death every day of your life. It puts your day into perspective. To that end I have a little trick up my sleeve that I have only recently acquired. Sim Scott, a cousin of mine, whom I used to visit on occasion to get away from the coalmine in South Shields when I worked there over thirty years ago (he lived nearby), got his call-up papers last year. Out of the blue the doctors diagnosed him with throat cancer and gave him three weeks and he died pretty punctually. A nicer guy you could not have met. His death haunts me just by the sheer surprise and swiftness of it and it has become a great aid to prayer. I imagine I am Sim and out of the blue I am told I have got three weeks to live. I won't make it out of the month. It puts what they call the fear of God in you and that helps to bring alive His presence. My sister, Arabella and her cousin, Hugh, both had cancer at the same time and they met that last summer and they both agreed that the prospect of death had effortlessly made God real for them – RIP the pair of them.

Then I call up my dearly departed sister, Arabella, whom I have made my own personal patron saint for families, and my father is the saint for businessmen. Arabella was such a family woman and my father made business such fun. To Arabella, I pray for any family member who might be temporarily going through a tough time and Dad, I put on suicide watch for my businesses that seem permanently to want to self-destruct.

The rest of my time I pray for grace by immersing myself in the imagined presence of God and Our Lady. Grace is a lightness of being and a readiness to be amused. We all know people of grace. Children in their innocence are full of grace. They alleviate a room.

I do not necessarily use words. Silence is useful but I also believe words are a very important part of prayer. You should strive for expression in your devotions.

Just one final point: Obviously the whole attempt at prayer is to try and pray successfully just like the idea of conversation is to have a good one but you should not beat yourself up about lacklustre prayer because of something very encouraging Cardinal Basil Hume wrote: 'Trying to pray is praying.'

Martin Luther King's Prayer

Do you want to hear the most amazing and heartfelt prayer I've ever been privileged enough to eavesdrop? Martin Luther King shared it in his autobiography. I am going to quote two whole pages of his book to put you in the picture so that you can fully appreciate the cause and effect of that prayer of his on the worst night of his life, the night he doubted himself near the start of the civil rights campaign that liberated America:

Almost immediately after the protest started we had begun to receive threatening telephone calls and letters. They increased as time went on. By the middle of January, they had risen to thirty and forty a day.

From the beginning of the protest both my parents and Coretta's parents always had the unconscious, and often conscious, fear that something fatal might befall us. They never had any doubt about the rightness of our actions but they were concerned about what might happen to us. My father made a beaten path between Atlanta and Montgomery throughout the days of protest. Every time I saw him I went through a deep feeling of anxiety, because I knew that my every move was driving him deeper and deeper into a state of worry. During those days he could hardly mention the many harassments that Coretta, the baby, and I were subjected to without shedding tears.

As the weeks passed, I began to see that many of the threats were in earnest. Soon I felt myself faltering and growing in fear. One day, a white friend told me that he had heard from reliable sources that plans were being made to take my life. For the first time I realised that something could happen to me.

One night at a mass meeting. I found myself saying: 'If one day you find me sprawled out dead, I do not want you to retaliate with a single act of vengeance. I urge you to continue protesting with the same dignity and discipline you have shown so far.' A strange silence came over the audience.

One night toward the end of January I settled into bed late, after a strenuous day, Coretta had fallen asleep and just as I was about to doze off the telephone rang. An angry voice said: 'Listen, nigger, we've taken all we want from you; before next week you'll be sorry you ever game to Montgomery.' I hung up, but I couldn't sleep. It seemed that all of my fears had come down on me at once. I had reached saturation point.

I got out of bed and began to walk the floor. I had heard these things before, but for some reason that night it got to me. I turned over and I tried to go to sleep, but I couldn't sleep. I was frustrated, bewildered, and then I got up. Finally, I went to the kitchen and heated a pot of coffee. I was ready to give up. With my cup of coffee sitting untouched before me I tried to think of a way to move out of the picture without appearing a coward. I sat there and thought about a beautiful little daughter who had just been born. I'd come in night after night and see that gentle little smile. I started thinking about a dedicated and loyal wife, who was over there asleep. And she could be taken from me, or I could be taken from her. And I got to the point that I couldn't take it any longer. I was weak. Something said to me: 'You can't call on Daddy now; you can't even call on Mama. You've got to call on that something in that person that your Daddy used to tell you about, that power that can make a way out of no way.' With my head in my hands, I bowed over the kitchen table and prayed aloud. 'Lord, I'm down here trying to do what's right. I think I'm right. I am here taking a stand for what I believe is right. But Lord, I must confess that I'm weak now. I'm faltering. I'm losing my courage. Now, I'm afraid. And I can't let the people see me like this because if they see me weak and losing my courage, they will begin to get weak. The people are looking at me for leadership and if I stand before them without strength and courage, they too will falter. I am at the end of my powers. I have nothing left. I've come to the point where I can't face it alone.'

It seemed as though I could hear the quiet assurance of an inner voice saying: 'Martin Luther, stand up for righteousness. Stand up for justice. Stand up for truth. And lo, I will be with you. Even until the end of the world.'

I tell you I've seen the lightning flash. I've heard the thunder roar. I've felt sin breakers dashing trying to conquer my soul. But I heard the voice of Jesus saying still to fight on. He promised never to leave me alone. At that moment I experienced the presence of the Divine, as I had never experienced Him before. Almost at once my tears began to go. My uncertainty disappeared. I was ready to face anything.

And are you telling me Martin Luther King is a liar? He's worth a thousand clever Amises.

The only other thing I can say is a tip from Shakespeare:

O limèd soul that, struggling to be free,
Art more engaged! Help, angels. Make assay.
Bow, stubborn knees, and, heart with strings of steel,
Be soft as sinews of the newborn babe.

You have to open your heart if you don't want to waste your time in prayer.

CHAPTER TEN

Backing Gammon

If you want to know the common ruck of humanity you need look no further than the *Titanic*. I mean I'm all for behaving sensibly in times of danger and it asks a lot of you to risk your life for another but that was not what was being asked of the survivors in their lifeboats after the *Titanic* had sunk. Yet hardly anybody did anything. There was a scene in the film where the first class passengers were safely ensconced in the lifeboats and they could hear people thrashing about in the freezing water screaming for help.

The camera zoomed in on one boat where the person with the biggest heart was having an argument with the person with the strongest head and all else were silent witnesses. This woman was advocating rescue and this man said it was impractical because the people in the water may well capsize them in their desperation to get into the boat. It must have been a genuine democratic decision because disaster had stripped away all rank. And it was not a panic decision because they had time enough to consider the options. Would they go to the rescue of their fellow man? On balance they thought they would rather not.

The obvious solution was to wait until most of the people in the sea were too weak to offer any resistance and then fish them out at their leisure. I would have got everybody in my boat to stand up to make room for as many extra people as possible. This would not have been much of an inconvenience because they all knew help was at hand. Distress flares had been discharged and emergency radio signals had been sent. Anybody can stand up for a couple of hours. Hell, I've queued for longer!

Now, here are the statistics. Only one boat of the twenty returned to save the dying people in the sea and some of the boats were only half full, such was the panic to leave the sinking liner and not to be sucked under with it. Out of the 1500 people who went down with the *Titanic* only six people were picked up from the freezing waters. And if you think that is just typical shoddy behaviour of the well-to-do, I will give you another statistic. Four out of five absent fathers do not contribute a penny to the cost of the upbringing of their children, their own flesh and blood – the people they must surely love above everybody else in the world. And if you think that is just the lower orders playing up as usual, I would draw your attention to Japanese behaviour in the last war. An entire army – which is as good a cross-section of society as you can ask – spent the war having sex with women without their consent. 'They said they couldn't help but do it because it was an order from their emperor,' wrote reporter Soon-Ae in the *Sunday Times* article of 7 January 2001. The Japanese government laid on 200,000 what they called 'comfort women' for members of their armed services to enjoy.

The article reported that these women used to service up to forty men per day. If you do the maths, you realise this industrial rape must have involved the entire Japanese army, navy and air force with little time left over for actual fighting. I wonder how many Japanese military turned down the offer of free sex: one per cent or none per cent?

'O that's just the Japanese, all that Far Eastern lot are cruel. Look at the Vietnamese and the Cambodians and as for the Indonesians, you should see the film: *The Act of Killing*,' says one of my barmen in Hootananny.

What about the Germans, a nation of philosophers? My father, who fought them in the last war, made no distinction between them and us. Given similar circumstances, Hitler could have happened here, he said. Personally, I think we would have been saved by our sense of humour. It gives us a sense of perspective, but he had seen enough in the war to disagree.

'There is no difference between a German soldier and a British soldier except a German will advance without air cover.'

'But surely,' I said to my father. 'If I had been a German soldier, I would have said to myself: "What on earth am I doing in somebody else's country shooting them up? This can't be right."'

'If you stick a uniform on somebody and give him a gun, he will use it no matter what country he is in.'

'What, even Greece?'

'Especially Greece, It's too hot. It makes you irritable, especially if you are weighed down with military clobber. I know. I was there with the Lovat Scouts,' he said. 'I am afraid to say civilisation is a thin veneer. Underneath it all, people are pretty basic.'

That is what the war had taught him. People are crap. Jesus Christ called them sheep. Obviously there are heroic exceptions, but few and far between. How many officers in the German army, for example, resigned their commissions after having barged into yet another country? I can see me saying to a fellow officer in the officer's mess over a shared Schnapps: 'That's enough. One more country and I'm off!'

Left to its own devices, human nature behaves badly, which tallies with the Christian doctrine of original sin. We are born bad. Maybe that overstates it. We are certainly born selfish. One look at a child tells you that. How do we get from that natural state to a point where we put other people before ourselves?

Of course, you know exactly what I am going to say. God is the answer. We know that with the best of intentions and the highest of ideals – you only have to look at a Communist regime – things go wrong incredibly quickly if a state turns its back on religion. Power is so profoundly corrupting that you need a huge counterweight to keep it in check.

You're Absolutely Wrong

You want to know how corrupting power can be? I'll give you a local example that is shocking because we take it for granted. It's the story of the brothers Miliband. They were brought up steeped in Socialist principles: equality and fraternity being two of them. *Frater* is the Latin for brother. Their father was a pedagogue of a Marxist.

David surprisingly loses the Labour Party leadership election to Ed. You would have thought he would have been delighted. It's his own brother. Obviously he would have preferred it to have been himself but surely your own brother winning is a good second-best. Quitting politics in a huff tells you he was only ever in it for the power. It gives the lie to his whole career.

If I had been David Miliband, I would have said to the press: 'I am not going to quit the shadow cabinet because my brother has won the leadership. It is not about him or me, it is about them, the people we represent, and they are lucky because they are going to get two Milibands for the price of one because I am right behind my brother every step of the way. How could you imagine for a moment I would not be overjoyed at my own brother's success? You the press are taking a liberty, us two brothers are the fraternity and our party believes in equality!'

Power addles the brain and riddles the regime. But in the grand scheme of things we notice that corruption is kept to manageable levels and state-sponsored murder really does not happen in Christian democracies. Even Islamic dictatorships are preferable to those dictatorships that operate without the effect of religion. Iran under the Ayatollah compared favourably to its neighbour, Iraq, under Saddam Hussein, for example. Internal oppression was a lot lower with less deaths and the Ayatollah did not go in for all this invading of other peoples' countries. If countries can behave badly with religion, they are far worse without it. Just think of the behaviour of all those Communist and Fascist countries in the last century.

It is the difference between absolute and relative morality. If you believe in the theory of relativity, the ends justify the means, especially in politics. In private life it starts in the wrong place. It starts with you. Other people are taken into consideration but they are not primary. So you can as a humanist, for example, commit adultery as long as you don't hurt other human beings. Discretion is the key. Forty per cent of all affairs are never discovered.

But then again, it just depends on your criterion. I am reading a book at the moment, *Talking It Over* by Julian Barnes: a classic tale about a fellow having fallen in love with his best friend's wife. This character, Oliver, turns to the reader and asks quite reasonably: 'O please take that disapproving look off your face . . . Would you renounce your love, slip gracefully from the scene, become a goatherd and play mournfully consoling music on your Panpipes all day while your heedless flock chomp the succulent tufts? People don't do that. People never did. Listen, if you go off and become a goatherd you never loved her in the first place.'

Oliver makes two assumptions. He has two criteria by which he judges his own behaviour. Love is King. Normality is God. That is just sloppy thinking. No other way to describe it and yet, at least Oliver's creator, Julian Barnes, is being honest – that is how atheists view adultery. It is just an unfortunate thing that people get caught up in and there is nothing much you can do about it. True love justifies the carnage. Incidentally, this in itself is nonsense because all adulterous love in its early stages is merely illusion because you hardly know the person. Saying everybody does it and it is the way of the world is just an abdication of responsibility. It certainly is not a moral code.

Somebody, who not only believes in God but carries out instructions to the letter, does the un-normal thing and removes himself from temptation or if he does run off with his best friend's wife, at least he does not excuse himself. Mitigating circumstances do not enter the equation. Thou shalt not commit adultery. It is there in black and white. That is the beauty of absolute morality. At least, you take your bad behaviour like a man.

Give Us a Break, God

Now that you have entered old age, you are aware of the limitations of the hedonistic lifestyle and you now have the chance to at least moderate your overwhelming desire for the good things of this world. That does not mean to say that you have to rush to the other extreme. As I keep on saying, I believe life is a balancing act. God is half the story. The other half is Man. Half the story is Love. The other half is Knowledge. The apple has been bitten. Hello sex. Hello money. Hello power. Hello alcohol. But you can drink without becoming an alcoholic.

The problem about God is that he appears to be incredibly un-compromising. He says you cannot be the servant of two masters: God and Mammon. Well, I am a firm believer in Gammon. We, who are not the clergy, have to live in this world and that involves engaging with Mammon. We have got to earn livings to pay for families. I think Jesus Christ was unnecessarily harsh with the well-intentioned rich man who very sensibly refused to give up his money to become a follower. Just imagine if you did that, what your wife would say and your descendants would curse you down the ages for having thrown away their inheritance. Imagine what this rich fellow said to his wife when he came home after meeting Christ.

'I have just met this excellent fellow who speaks an awful lot of sense. He is a joiner from Kiltarlity. Knocks around with people from the docks. He guarantees life after death.'

'Why on earth should you believe him? Who on earth does he think he is that he can say that?

'I am not sure "on earth" is the right expression. "In heaven" is more like it.'

'And he is a joiner . . . from Kiltarlity!'

'Well, that's more his day job and everybody has got to come from somewhere.'

'Yes, but Kiltarlity!'

'Poetry is made up of perfectly ordinary words.'

'So is bullshit.'

'He is inspiring. He is mesmerising. He performs miracles. What he says cuts through the crap. I offered my services.'

'What?'

'You don't need to worry. He turned me down or rather I turned him down. He said I had to give away all my money if I wanted to work for him.'

'Well, thank God, you're not a complete fool!'

My sympathies are with the wife. I had had a several times great-great-great-grandfather who gave away his priceless art collection, the nucleus of which was looted by his grandfather during the Napoleonic wars. He gave it to an Oxford University college which I applied to get in as an undergraduate but they turned me down due to lack of brains. Just one of those pictures would have got me in if only he had not impulsively given them all away 150 years ago. If only he had allowed his descendants to drip feed them one at a time in exchange for individual admission. Instead my grandmother had to invite the tutor for admissions for politics at Bristol University to a cocktail party at her stately home in Gloucestershire to get me in there. That's a poor second.

However, I accept that money can be an obstacle to salvation but it is surely not insurmountable. Freud has liberated all taboo about sex, drugs have been normalised and the pubs stay open till three in the morning. There is so much pleasure now currently available, vicariously and in reality, it seems a waste not to get some of it and why should that exclude also having a real relationship with the Lord?

Of course, it doesn't but pleasure needs handling with care. Money needs to be a by-product of work, not the primary motivation. Sex should be uninhibited but within an exclusive relationship. Drink should only be used to oil the wheels of social encounter. Maybe the right place for drugs is in a religious ceremony, as they are used in tribal society.

Kingsley Amis devoted his entire life's literary work to the study of money, drink and sex. He made great comedy out of the hilarious situations his protagonists get themselves into via their exclusive pursuit of these three primary forms of pleasure. He showed how it hollowed out a person and left him in despair but he could not see an alternative way to live. He applauded his characters for at least being honest. The means had become the ends but there were no ends, was his accurate conclusion from the point of view of an atheist.

Scientists test theories in the laboratory by taking extreme cases – that way the results show up more clearly. Kingsley Amis and Jean Vanier are two extreme cases. They were both extremely bright young men who had the capacity to live life to the full and squeeze every last ounce of meaning out of it. Amis devoted his life exclusively to Mammon and Vanier to God. Let us test their theories of life because it will have had an effect on them. How did they fare? How did they end up as old men?

I have spent the sum total of twenty minutes with Jean Vanier, just the two of us in a room and I can vouch for the effect he has on you. It is one of huge relaxation. You do not realise how stressed you are until you meet him because the tension falls off your shoulders. He absolutely emanates the power of goodness. It is holiness; nothing pious about it at all. He is so ready to be amused and a smile is never far from his lips and yet unlike with a powerful and charismatic man of the world like a prime minister or a film star, you are the opposite of nervous and tongue-tied. You feel as if you are with somebody who has love (as in real affection) for you and yet he has only just met you.

I will tell you one story about him. Women sometimes are attacked by the feeling they are never going to get married. They can feel left on a shelf. They can feel life passing them by. A friend of my sister, Sophia, Maggie Parrin was only thirty-two but that didn't make any difference to how she was feeling. There are two things you ought to know about Maggie. She is very devout and she is very clever. These attributes do not necessarily recommend themselves to men on the pull. We love daft, sinful blondes.

The final straw was when her flat mate was getting married. As a last resort she thought she might go to the L'Arche Centre in France to see if she had a vocation for looking after the disabled. She stayed a month and decided it was not for her. On the train journey north to Paris she found herself in tears when just two stops before Paris, who should get on to the train and come and sit down right beside her but the founder of L'Arche himself, Jean Vanier. He immediately asked her what was wrong. She told him about her foolishness. He comforted her for forty-five minutes before the train got into Paris and then he said he would pray for her. She got back home in the UK to a phone call from her flat mate inviting her to the country for the weekend. The newly married couple had decided to invite their two greatest friends for their first social weekend as man and wife. By Saturday night Maggie knew she had met her future husband, Jamie Ferguson, and sure enough they subsequently got married. Many months later she met Jean Vanier again and told him about the amazing results of his prayers. 'I know. I have a gift,' he said simply. It has been given to him by God but he has earned his gift.

I have never met Kingsley Amis but I will take the evidence of his biographer, Eric Jacobs, who gave this snapshot of him. 'There is something childish about Kingsley, literally. His face reflects his feelings, like a child's. He does nothing for himself. I'm pretty certain he doesn't lift a finger to help around the Thomas's' house [where he lived]. There is something childish, too, in his appetites. I don't say he would cry if he didn't get his drink or food when he wanted them but you can't help feeling he might. He guzzles, like a child sucking a tit. And he is not happy with strangers or with anything that threatens to take him out of his normal routines. You have to win acceptance and you must play things his way, e.g., drink and eat according to his schedule, or he will get bored, petulant. And he has to be entertained constantly – by books, people, television. None of this is meant to distract from his great qualities: wit, intelligence and a lot more.'

Let me give you another comparison. Hunter S. Thompson was a cultural icon, a young man's hero like Che Guevara for people trying to shake themselves free of *The System*, as it used to be called in the Sixties. He was the rat that escaped the laboratory. Here was a crazy, bohemian, free-thinking, drink and drug fiend of a chaos warrior who could do what he liked and say and wrote what he wanted and knew how to Live the Life in capital letters. He invented gonzo journalism which put you at the centre of your reportage and allowed you to cobble together any old crap you wanted in a stream of consciousness that overwhelmed the reader with the power of its free association. To make it work you too had to be totally free. That made you spontaneous. Personal liberation came from realising one fundamental fact and taking it to its ultimate conclusion. There were no rules because God was a concept dreamed up by the Establishment just to keep you in your place, man.

That was the legend and philosophy and style of Hunter S. Thompson but I think personally, while obviously having talent and energy in abundance, he was a grossly self-indulgent egotist of epic proportions and an adolescent right up to the day he killed himself. He thought he was great when he wrote: 'Life should not be a journey to the grave with the intention of arriving safely in a pretty and well preserved body, but rather to skid in broadside in a cloud of smoke, thoroughly used up, totally worn out and loudly proclaiming: "Wow! What a ride!"' And not sparing a thought for anyone else, he should have added. He was basically advocating the rock and roll life style. I have met a few people in later life who have tried to follow his example and they ended up hollow shells.

It is not so superficially as attractive as his clarion call to party but I subscribe more to the view that the twin purpose of life is the pursuit of love and knowledge so that you go to your grave a man with a big heart and great understanding, having fulfilled your potential to the betterment of your fellow man. My philosophy of life does not preclude parties. It is based on loving yourself as well as other people. As I say it is Gammon which means that God is half the story. Otherwise it is just Mammon and we see where that gets people, especially in old age. You must now have realised that whatever the world offered you has proven to be illusory. 'Is that it?' you say to yourself. Perhaps you should consider the alternative to Mammon.

Certainly my typical English moderate, compromised, in the best sense of the word, middle of the road, nothing too arduous, almost Anglican approach to happiness has not worked. My Golden Mean method to the God and Mammon dichotomy: what I have called Gammon, has not made me particularly happy. It has just dealt with unhappiness. I can honestly say that I am not unhappy, but that is not the same as being happy.

I feel slightly compromised by possibly having overdone the Mammon. I am by nature rather self-indulgent. I am very treat-orientated. I suppose what I am saying is that I don't think I got the balance quite right. The Mammon mostly got the better of the God. So maybe it is not the theory that is flawed but me. I should really have upped the God bit of the equation and then it might have worked. My new mantra is: 'The more the Mammon, the more the God.'

Ten years ago I wrote in my diary:

I am not one of those amazing people who give up their lives to become priests. I am just like you: a muddled mixture in the middle, thinking life is tough enough having to do a thousand things a day for other people just to earn a living, not to treat yourself on occasion to a bit of bad behaviour. A little light sinning is surely good for the digestion, just to vary the diet.

I am susceptible to women and prone to drink. I am saved from what I call bad sex through consideration for others and fear of retribution. Bad boozing, which is drink for oblivion, is not easy in the country due to draconian drink driving laws. So sex for me is reduced to wrongful flirtation and circumstances keep a lid on my nascent alcoholism. The result is that life feels like constant effort, punctuated with little satisfactions and occasional bursts of pleasure.

There is another way of living which feels totally different. It feels constantly light and amusing. You feel really good inside: just easy, natural and calm, in a word: cool – the one thing youth makes a God of. They know instinctively it is the one thing that matters. Cool is more important than wealth and fame. What creates real cool is a thing called grace: the product of prayer. Why pray? It makes you cool.

I need to get into good habits of mind. Bed at 10. Up at 6. Cut out late night TV and replace it with early morning prayers to set you up for the day. And don't drink during the week. It is all to do with nurturing the spirit. Prayer feeds the spirit and drink dissipates it. Reserve drink for parties to give you a heightened and temporary sense of communion with other people. That is good use of drink, recommended I think by the Lord who changes his blood into wine at Holy Communion.

Now alone in old age, I can turn those resolutions into actuality. A resolution is only as good as its implementation and if you have read my trilogy there is nobody better than me at resolutions. I think I have been waiting all my life for old age to arrive so that I can finally implement my finely tuned resolutions. I have now got nobody and nothing to distract me. Postponement is history!

The other option to the Gammon approach to life is humanism. What a humanist does is replace God with Love. He says stuff like: 'What gives my life meaning are my friends and family.' Listen to what an intelligent secular man like A. A. Gill says of the Miliband brothers: 'They are still young enough to think that ambition is everything. They will live to realise that, in fact, it matters little, and that your family and friends are close to everything.' I am sure A. A. Gill thought the same as the Milibands when he was their age but when he gets older still, he himself will realise that there is something even more important than family and friends. A clue is to be found in old age because it is just these two categories of people by whom you are abandoned. The postman comes round every day, not your son or daughter.

Most people like A. A. Gill think that the solution to loneliness is the company of other people but that overlooks the fact that although old age is fundamentally a solitary experience, it does not necessarily have to be lonely. By the time you have reached retirement age, you have long since lost regular contact with your bosom buddies of youth and the guys at work disappear the moment you leave the office. You see your grown-up children at Christmas and Easter and maybe a week over the summer and your husband or wife is either dead, divorced or disinterested. Come on, let's be honest. What do you think of Edith Goldman's view of marriage as a bourgeois institution designed for comfort rather than life? Edith Goldman is the socialist revolutionary in E. L. Doctorow's *Ragtime* and she is advising Younger Brother to get over having been dumped by the actress, Evelyn Nisbett. 'You're a bourgeois; you would want to marry her. You would destroy each other inside of a year. [Most people's interest in one another lasts longer, I suggest: Ed] You would see her begin to turn old and bored under your very eyes. You would sit across the dinner table from each other in bondage, in terrible bondage to what you thought was love.' I think she is describing a lot of marriages that really quite quickly descend into a sort of fearful and asphyxiating co-dependency. I think probably loneliness is as common in a marriage as out of one. So we are all prey to it.

'In a world where the computer replaces human encounter and psychology replaces religion, it is no wonder that there is an obsession with relationship. Unfortunately, however, relationship has become an empty centre around which our lonely hunger forages for warmth and belonging,' wrote John O'Donohue. 'Real intimacy is a sacred experience. Real intimacy is of the soul and the soul is reserved.'

CHAPTER ELEVEN

Cramming for your Finals

I have lived my home life surrounded by people, coming from a family of six and breeding one of my own of four. Then, in the latter part of the marriage, people started to thin out. One by one my three older children went off to university and then my wife went off with the neighbour and finally, my youngest child, Calum went off to Australia at the start of his gap year. And so finally it was just me and the dog. I never wanted the dog. I don't even like dogs.

Julie, who is the dog, took advantage of me. She used to climb onto the furniture, for example, something she was never allowed to do under the old order, and watch television with me. She ate handsomely from my leftovers because I had lost my appetite. She got to chase sheep on more than one occasion, through my absent-mindedness and there's nothing she likes better than doing that. She would climb onto my bed and sleep with me half the time. One of my low points was waking up one morning, imagining before consciousness had fully kicked in, that I still had a wife. I put my arms round this warm but unfortunately furry body. What woke me up with a start was the feel of Julie's wet nose on my dry one.

Then there came the fateful night when I put my foot down. I was fed up with the bloody animal and I made sure I shut the door of the sitting room with it in it when I went to bed. I tried to block my ears to its canine requests to come and join me. Admittedly I did notice its whining was particularly heart-rending, but the dog is a natural born tragedian. It plays on the heart strings like Yehudi Menuin. I would like to say I won the battle of wills with Julie but she got the better of me and I found myself padding through to the sitting room. I stuck her in the car out of earshot.

Next day I had a nice leisurely breakfast in peace and I ambled through to the sitting room and thought something annoying was missing. Then I remembered the dog. I rushed to the car to let it out for a pee. Julie had objected to her imprisonment and the sight that greeted me was what authorities' term: 'a dirty protest'. On second thoughts, it occurred to me the reason Julie had been so particularly vocal the previous night was because she had been trying to tell me that she felt the imminence of diarrhoea and was clamouring to be let out into the garden.

I phoned a car valeting firm in Inverness and explained my predicament and asked them whether they would clean the inside of my car if it was splattered with the dog diarrhoea. The East European at the reception desk, who later I thought was perhaps not familiar with the word, did not seem to think that would be a problem. So I travelled at speed, with both windows open, to Inverness. The car valets, if I maybe be so gallant as to call them that, took one look at the disgusting spectacle of my car interior and refused to clean it. So I had an equally horrible return journey. Rather than throw away the car, I cleaned it out myself with bleach and fairy liquid about 20 times over the next two months to get rid of every last trace of the appalling smell. The first thing I did on my return, however, was to phone my wife and say: 'I divorce the dog.'

And – to give her her due – she came and collected it that day and has looked after it ever since.

Goodbye Dog. Hello God.

The Great Thing about being by Yourself is You don't have to Talk to Anybody

Ah, the joys of solitude, the great gift of old age. I can inhabit a home. I can wander around a room, lost in my thoughts. I can lie on my bed and grab some sleep. 'Cooker', I say, 'Cooker, cook and it cooks.' I can go up those stairs and then I can come down them. 'Bath, my little beauty, I will bare myself naked and lie in thy spaciousness.' And I can toil on the toilet and not answer the phone. Treats, pleasures and privileges I accord myself as private reward for effort expended, but the chief comfort is my imaginary friend. There is no other person to barge into my consciousness and shatter the illusion. I say: illusion, not delusion, note. God is currently sitting in the armchair opposite.

The solitude of old age is a perfect opportunity to get to know God. I do whole shifts of 24 or even 36 hours without seeing anybody now. By the second night in bed, when I can't get to sleep for lack of exercise and no drink, because like most people I never drink by myself, I feel nice and lonely in a good way and in He comes like a welcome ghost. Actually the devil is easier to imagine. It is not difficult to spook yourself in bed. It is not difficult to give yourself nightmares. Just do the opposite.

Switch off the TV and switch on the imagination. Frighten yourself in the dark with thoughts of death. Practice your essential loneliness. These are the right conditions for an awareness of His presence. If you have not spoken to anyone in a day and a half, it is a small step to start chatting to an imaginary friend and you have no greater friend in the world than God and no greater call on your imagination – whatever it takes to conjure up the Lord. That is the point of Mass. It is our ritualised version of what tribes of natives do, dancing and chanting around a fire in the dead of night.

Why They say Silence is Golden

The other priceless gift of old age is silence. It is what should happen when we are not with other people but then a lot of us try and immediately fill up the gap with mechanical noise of one sort or another emanating from the television or the radio or some other sound system. But we miss out on so much if we block out the experience of silence. The other world is silent.

When we go to sleep and enter the other world, we drop into silence. Dreams – which the scientists of human behaviour, the psychologists, inform us – are when our subconscious tells us the truth about ourselves if only we can accurately decipher their symbolism, happen in silence. Secrets are whispered. It is almost as if the more important the information, the quieter the communication. Money merely rustles. Power insists on hush. The universe at large exists in a state of silence and our own world is mostly silent so that it is all the more shocking when it occasionally makes a noise.

All the big moments in your life are conducted in near enough silence. When the sperm first penetrates the egg in the deepest, darkest part of the womb and you first come into being, not even the most microscopic microphone can pick up so much as a blip of sound. And when you were born, the noise you made coming out of the tunnel of love will have been a slurp and a gurgle and then the silence before your first cry.

Your first sight of the woman you will eventually marry will come with the speed of light but no sound. When you are married at the altar of love, you will not hear the golden wedding ring being slipped over your brand new wife's third finger. And when you die, it will not be with a bang but a whimper – unless, of course, you have just been shot.

The arts are created in silence. Every book that there has ever been written has been battled out by its author wrestling with his or her mind in silence. I am in a mental punch-up right now and you can't hear a thing. Have you heard the sound of paint going on to a canvas? Perhaps a little dabbing noise if it's oils. Watercolours are seamless. Great rock anthems, amplified in a decibel count mega enough for football stadia full of people to feel them through their bodies, are penned in such quiet.

Expertise, which is a million words, comes from the city but wisdom, the stuff of silence, comes essentially from nature. Every creature in the world lives mostly in silence. Silence is one of the three great monoliths of existence, along with time and space. God is silent.

Stillness is Difficult

The central point of the hub of the wheel does not move. When you are young and attempting to be a dashing young man in your social life or a whiz kid in your field of work, you are operating at the outermost rim of the wheel. The job of life is to centre yourself and certainly when you reach old age, you should have developed an appetite for stillness which gives you the perfect environment for reflection.

Prayer, which is good preparation for old age, is an exercise in stillness. People who are not used to prayer suffer from a desperate urge to get up from their knees and move about after a very short period of time.

'The longest and most exciting journey is the journey inwards,' writes John O'Donohue in *Anam Cara* and for that you need solitude, peace and stillness and old age affords the time, environment and opportunity.

My father lived in a castle surrounded by family and employees. We all took part in Highland Wineries which made country wines, coolies, sauces and jellies like Elderflower, Meadowsweet and Silver Birch wines and Horseradish and Dill sauces in the castle out-buildings and the shop that sold our twenty or so products was attached, in the wing of the castle. Dad would sit in an armchair in the kitchen smoking Hamlet cigars and occasionally treating himself to a gin and tonic. That was his throne and he was the king and he did not have to move because all life poured through that kitchen with its four doors: North, South, East and West. He mostly sat there chuckling away, very ready to be entertained and we came to him always with our best stories. He loved the business, nurtured it and counted the money at the end of each working day. He was a dynamic young man, commanding his regiment, the Lovat Scouts at the tender age of twenty-six. He was a powerful man in his prime with a family of six whom he successfully provided for. But now in old age he just sat in his armchair in the kitchen with plenty of time to reflect on things in the bosom of his community. The only time I saw him stir from his chair with any sense of urgency was when word came to him one time that there were two lesbians in the castle shop.

'Get me up, get me up, help me along, couple of people I have got to see in the shop!' he shouted. He didn't think lesbians existed. Incidentally, he was very tottery on his feet and he arrived a moment too late and they had gone. 'There you are,' he said. 'Nobody!'

Where the Hell Are You?

Invisibility is the other mystery you have time in old age to contemplate as you yourself gradually disappear with people paying less and less notice of you until eventually there comes the day when you actually vanish from the world.

When I told my children about God and the Devil, and Holy Communion at bedtime when I could have their undivided attention, I gave Angie and Vita nightmares and Calum, an asthma attack. Sandy's dreams were too heavy populated with footballers for the Devil to be accommodated.

I had to tell them about the invisible world. I told them about the power of the spirit and how the Host might look just like a wafer but once transubstantiated became the body of Christ and the wine became His blood. 'O you Catholics are so literal,' is the usual refrain. 'No, we have imagination,' is my answer. And I could tell from the widening eyes of my kids that they were proper little Catholics.

I told them we got power in the form of grace from God when we took his spirit into ourselves by taking Communion. I talked about holiness. I said there were holy people who had a powerful effect on anybody who came across them, and conversely there were evil people possessed by the Devil, also very powerful and they were frightening.

The Mass is how we summon up God. I said Satanists also have ceremonies to summon up Satan. Being children, of course, they were much more interested in the Devil and other baddies. Inevitably Satan got back at them later that night in their dreams. In that respect they were like Milton but he could play out his dreams in his poetry.

Hitler Meets Satan

I came across an amazing book in my father's library, called *Hitler Speaks* by Hermann Rauschning, who was one of Hitler's innermost circle in the 1930s, before he quit in disgust when he grasped the true nature of the man and what was being planned. This book was not published in the UK till 1939 and went through five reprints in as many months. The book's primarily a record of scores of conversations he had with Hitler in 1933 and 1934, outlining how Hitler intended first to create Greater Germany out of Austria, Czechoslovakia and half of Poland, ally and then double-cross the Soviet Union, beat France, take over Europe and then, unbelievably, the world. America was on his hit list because there were more Americans from German descent than British. This fifth column would be easily mobilised.

He also gives us a glimpse into Hitler's private life and we discover that even the most atheist of men cannot escape the world of the spirit:

His sleeplessness is more than the mere result of excessive nervous strain. He often wakes up in the middle of the night and wanders restlessly to and fro. Then he must have the light everywhere. Lately he has sent at these times for young men who have to keep him company during these hours of manifest anguish. A man in the closest daily association with him gave me this account: Hitler wakes at nights with convulsive shrieks. He shouts for help. He sits on the edge of his bed, as if unable to stir. He shakes with fear, making the whole bed vibrate. He shouts confused, totally unintelligible phrases. He gasps, as if imagining himself to be suffocating.

My informant described to me in full detail a remarkable scene – I should not have credited the story if it had not come from such a source. Hitler stood swaying in his room, looking wildly about him. 'He! He! He's been here!' he gasped. His lips were blue. Sweat streamed down his face. Suddenly he began to reel off figures, and odd words and broken phrases, entirely devoid of sense. It sounded horrible. He used strangely composed and entirely unGerman word-formations. Then he stood quite still, only his lips moving. He was massaged and offered something to drink. Then he suddenly broke out – 'There. There! In that corner! Who's that?'

He stamped and shrieked in the familiar way. He was shown there was nothing out of the ordinary in the room, and then he gradually grew calm. After that he lay asleep for many hours, and then for some time things were endurable.

Old Age is God's Revenge

If Death is Land's End, Old Age is Penzance. Penance more like. You have made most of the mistakes you are going to make and now you have got to start making amends. You are getting to the end of the line and you are drinking in The Last Chance Saloon. It is like the train is leaving Penzance, and the voice above you over the intercom system is saying: 'Next stop: Death.'

That, as they say, concentrates the mind wonderfully. It sure relativises time and it puts your life into perspective. About a year before my father died, out of the blue, he suddenly made a spiritual confidence in me. This was extraordinary because being an old-fashioned country gent belonging to the wartime generation, he never talked about these things. Religion was bad form. You did or you didn't do religion but what you didn't do was talk about it – any more than you talked about your sex life.

He said: 'I had a dream last night that God was sitting opposite me at the dining room table and he asked me what I thought I had done in my life that would earn me a place in heaven. Well, I thought and I couldn't really think of anything much and then eventually God came round to my side of the table and helped me out.'

The only other death I have witnessed first hand was that of my sister, Arabella. She had cancer over seven years so there was a long lead up to it and plenty of opportunity to observe her coming to terms with death. Of course, she fought it every inch of the way enduring the normal tortures like chemo, radiotherapy and steroids. Her primary motivation was her children. She was desperately worried that they would be damaged by her premature death. She had a deep desire to see her daughter, Vanessa, safely married and she yearned herself for the wonderful experience of having grandchildren. 'O I do want some granchers!' she would say. She lived in hope and to that end she went on religious pilgrimages, one to Medjugorje and two to Lourdes.

I agree with the fellow who said about greatness that some people are born great, some become great and some people just have greatness thrust upon them. I think that is also true of sanctity. Some people quite frankly just pop out of the womb like that. They are blooming angels as children. They scoot through adolescence unnoticed and they blossom into amazing mothers, wives or spinsters, die and go back to where they came from, which was heaven. Everybody who ever met Arabella, at whatever age, knows that was true of her.

I am not claiming special status for my family because I bet most families if you take in uncle, aunts, nephews and nieces have at least one saint in their midst. Pope John Paul II made this point. He said saints are not rare. It is just that the Church do not have the manpower to recognise all the hundreds of thousands of holy people in the world. On his visit to the UK, Pope Benedict told primary school children to try and become saints. It required as much training and self-discipline as becoming a professional footballer but it had one advantage, You didn't need any talent.

Arabella died while I was taking a bath. Her husband, Joshua, knocked on my door and told me she had 'passed on'. Just then I wished he had said 'died'. I hate euphemisms for bald facts but then when I rushed down stairs and looked at her body, I felt he was right in what he had said. She had not died so much as gone; passed on to somewhere else. Where to? Probably the corner of the room. 'The dead are not far away, they are very, very near us.' wrote John O'Donohue. But wherever she was, she was definitely not in the body lying on that bed. That was a hollow shell. A piece of meat. It was no longer Arabella.

Do you know there is an activity called dying? Arabella had been dying all week. She was resigned to death only in this final period. A few days before she admitted she was dying, which was why we could all come down from Scotland and up from London to be at her death bed. She was gradually withdrawing from her body.

In the last week of her life, Arabella did a couple of strange things in phone calls to her sister-in-law, Mary. She groaned after every breath, Mary reported to us, and said: 'Who is that?' 'Who is making that noise?' And the other strange thing Arabella did was to start singing in the middle of the phone call, as if it was nothing to do with her, as if somebody else was singing, someone other than the person making the phone call. She was becoming disembodied. Her soul, or her Self, was beginning the process of disengaging from her body that would culminate in her actual full departure at the point of death by the end of the week.

Death only comes home to you when it happens to somebody

close to you of your own generation. It is only then you realise your own mortality. You are on a timer. It is massive and you had better start preparing for it. Death is actually the point of life. You should start with death and work backwards. It is only at funerals that you fully realise that you are remembered not for your wealth, your dominance or your success at work but for your ability to arouse love in others. It is always at a funeral that I am reminded of the words at the start of my second favourite musical of all time, Baz Lurhman's *Moulin Rouge* where the narrator says: 'The greatest thing is to learn to love and be loved in return.'

Arabella's death proved the success of her life. You only knew it at the end of her life because it is only at the end of a person's life that you can sum it up. It is only at the end that you could recognise the patterns of her life and its meaning.

Old age has got primarily to be a preparation for death, to set your house in order and try to correct the wrongs of the past and get yourself in the right frame of mind to meet your Maker. It's like cramming for your finals. I only seriously worked for my degree in the last couple of months when fear took over. The rest of my time at university was a joy ride.

People can change a hell of a lot in old age. People can gain a lovely humorous air of resignation, a mellowness and a sort of general affection for people: glad just for the attention. I love the way the right kind of old person is anything but censorious. You know how disapproving people are. All you are doing is trying your best and people jump on your mistakes and they are so quick to misinterpret you. Old people are no longer in competition with the world so they can afford to be generous. Isn't it great to come across some old geezer with a knowing smile on his face as if to say: 'Listen chum, don't beat yourself up about it, I've done worse.'

Animal, Vegetable, Mineral

As a baby you start off as a vegetable. Then you should become an animal with the full vigour of youth, in the bosom of your community, brimming with testosterone or estrogen according to your sex, energy and hubris. This should be followed by a severe knockback as you come to realise the full extent of your limitations which should temporarily send you back to the vegetable stage before scraping yourself off the floor, dusting yourself down and re-entering the fray. You come to terms with your insecurities and inadequacies and return to the animal state but this time armed with a certain amount of self-knowledge for double the fun. The final stage, which comes with the dismantling effect of age and the growth of genuine feeling for others, often the by-product of irreversible misfortune and failure, is spirituality.

Particularly dangerous and life denying are vegetables who become spiritual: all those timid people coming out of churches up and down the country like dead men walking on Sunday. You must first be an animal to become spiritual. Religion is based on three liquids: not just water but also wine and blood.

Of course, there is nothing better than an animal at the altar, a powerful person genuflecting. I remember what moved me most when I saw Pope Benedict pass me in his PopeMobile, practically within touching distance, at a huge gathering in Glasgow and a big bruiser of a working man shouted behind me in his gravelly Glaswegian: 'God Save The Pope!' It unaccountably moved me. Christianity was originally a working-class movement, not the respectable little white collar enclave it is now in the West.

But we can't all be working-class heroes. I personally belong to the pariah section of society called Country Toffs but even within my limited range I should express the animal in me by the vigour of my youth and the prime of my manhood before settling down to old age and the struggle for the salvation of my soul. This is a list of

'Fifty things a man of my ilk should have done in his life' that I knocked up with a couple of fellow toffs. These are our particular fantasies. We had all three done at least half of these things.

1) Own a snooker table.
2) Score a hat-trick of goals at any game, at any level.
3) Play in a pub band.
4) Spend a night in a police cell.
5) Have a car crash.
6) Be a barman.
7) Go to bed with a black woman. (White, if you are black)
8) Catch a salmon.
9) Ride a Harley Davidson.
10) Go bungee jumping.
11) Get buggered at boarding school.
12) Go to a casino in Monte Carlo.
13) Write an unpublished novel.
14) Be thrown out of home by your parents.
15) Have a punch-up in a bar.
16) Utterly fail at a project.
17) Drink a yard of ale.
18) Have sex outdoors.
19) Tell your boss to fuck off.
20) Be an extra in a movie.
21) Do the Highland Cross. (20 miles on foot, 30 miles on a bike)
22) Embarrass your daughter in front of her boyfriend.
23) Be a teenage rebel.
24) Wake up in bed with someone you don't recognise.
25) Get slapped in the face by a woman.
26) Have a dangerous animal as a pet.
27) Almost drown.
28) Go to a prostitute in Paris.

29) Consider suicide.

30) Totally cock-up a public speech.

31) Streak.

32) Have a restaurant meal without paying.

33) Gone bust.

34) Get a sexual disease.

35) Break a leg.

36) See a ghost.

37) Laugh at a funeral.

38) Run away from school or get expelled.

39) Score a century at cricket.

40) Do 24 hours without sleep and without drugs.

41) Walk out of an exam.

42) Be on the telly.

43) Snog a celebrity.

44) Jump out of a window.

45) Be mugged.

46) Get an erection in a hospital with a nurse present.

47) Get a right and a left. (pheasant or grouse)

48) Bunch a girl with a bouquet.

49) Fall asleep at a critical moment.

50) Holiday in a war zone.

CHAPTER TWELVE

Old Age: Time to Reconsider

'I'm reviewing the situation' famously sings Fagin in the musical, *Oliver*, contemplating in his old age a change of direction in his life now that his current métier was encountering severe difficulties. Old age is an opportunity to review situations in your life to date. Now that you are shot free of the battle zone, you have got the peace and quiet to reconsider the major incidents of your life and see it from the other person's point of view.

The biggest thing to happen in my life was my divorce. Originally I put the marriage breakdown to a misdiagnosis. There are four types of wife: Decorative Doormat, Worldly Woman, Freedom Fighter and Mother Nun. When I proposed to Sarah in the first place, I had obviously miss-categorised her.

Her actual infidelities I quite simply put down to the fact that she fell in love with other people and that I was blameless. I was comforted by my friends and my social circle who said she was just a social climber. 'You can take the girl out of Bishop's Stortford but not the Bishop's Stortford out of the girl,' they said. She had started life in rented accommodation and ended up with a couple of mansions and a very rich second husband, the son of a lord. But even then I disagreed. I said that it was not money and position that captivated her, it was power and beauty and the three guys she preferred to me had more of those two qualities. The first guy was actually an accented musician of modest means.

Otherwise, I was in denial. It is only in the calmer waters of old age that I can actually absorb what has gradually emerged about my part in the break-up of our marriage and admit responsibility.

The nicer type of adulterer, which I think Sarah was, presumably tries to soften the blow of the betrayal as much as possible and seeks to protect the poor fall guy from the full impact of the truth. The male ego is a fragile thing at the best of times. So when I myself, the traumatised goon, asked with bewilderment: 'Where did I go wrong? What's wrong with me?' Sarah just muttered something about my inadequacy in the field of household repairs. 'DIY' she said. 'You can barely change a plug.'

'Is that it?' I said.

This was not to last though. Word came through the grapevine that I had not done the washing up. I have to own up to this crime. In my defence, she never had a job. I had to earn all the money. So I thought that was a fair distribution of labour. On the subject of money, it soon came percolating through that a big problem about marriage to me had been my lack of a steady income. I was not a salaried man, as such. She privately had suffered agonies from an all pervading sense of financial insecurity. 'He saw money as something to gamble our future with. He was a typical man. He saw money in terms of adventure. As a woman, I see it as security.' Yes, it did not take long to be third-personned.

Then I heard from yet another helpful source that Sarah had complained about our weekly candle lit dinners when, so often with sufficient drink having been taken, conversation would degenerate into a monologue from me.

The next stage post in the dawning of the Age of the Aquarium with me drowning in it was a couple of years after what I called the Time of Cholera when for three weeks immediately after I had been told about her infidelities, and we had half a dozen sessions of supposed soul-baring enquiry as to what the hell had been going on in our marriage, I heard from possibly a fourth, fifth or sixth party that she had found it a relief being with my replacement, Kim, who was a proper man while I was stuck in a stage of arrested development, what Jung, Robert Bly and many others called the *puer aeternus* — the eternal boy — somebody who in some fundamental way had failed to grow up. It is all a question of interpretation. What she describes as adolescent, I might call enthusiastic.

Then a couple of years after that word got to me that Sarah's psychotherapist had described me as a narcissist which I gather is a particularly nasty thing to be.

Could it get worse than that? Yes, of course, it could. I only had to bide my time before being accused of wife beating. This referred to a physical exchange that took place when in The Time of Cholera I had repeatedly asked Sarah to answer what I regarded the Ultimate Question any adulterer should ask him or herself before adultering. 'How can you take your pleasure on the back of your children's pain?' She had left the table and rushed up to the bedroom, which only had one door and I stood in the way blocking her exit and said: 'You owe me an answer.' She rushed at me to try and get through me to escape and I picked her up and threw her onto the bed, which I thought was quite considerate in the heat of the moment: Soft landings. She then tried to leave by the window on the left and then by the window on the right. Both times I saved her from serious injury by tossing her back onto the bed. That was the sum total of our wrestling match.

Then, after six solid years since the break-up I got the final *coup de grâce*. I have heard from my Russian neighbour, Shenka, last night that Sarah had told her only a couple of weeks ago that quite early on in the marriage she had realised she had made a terrible mistake in marrying me in the first place. There was a basic social incompatibility in that like all male Frasers of my generation, in my extended family, beneath my showman's bluster lurked a spirit shy to the point of mild Asperger's, making me eschew society in favour of close encounter, thus denying her the right of all beautiful women which is to shine in public.

Shenka said Sarah had told her that she had only not left me because she kept on having babies. It was a remark that made my whole marriage a sham when I thought only half of it was a fake. It wiped out my adult past and buried my memories.

I was the wrong guy for her, she said, which explained her decade of infidelity. She was just trying to find the right guy. As the Cistercian monk, Erasmo Loira Merikas, wrote: 'If a married person feels that within the marriage she lacks what she was made for; it is unavoidable that the spouse will be perceived as an obstacle to happiness and this happiness will inevitably and understandably be sought elsewhere.'

With all this catalogue of complaint the wonder is not that she left me but that she stayed with me for as long as she did, even well beyond the Period of Pregnancies. Perhaps her comment to Mary Quinn, my bookkeeper just weeks before the marriage ended, held the key: 'The problem is he is my best friend,' she had said.

Still, in the cloudiest sky, there is always a silver lining. My children all agree that they now get much more attention from us. All the time Sarah and I used to devote to one another is now redirected towards them.

Nevertheless, I have to admit I found it quite difficult to get out of my bed this morning such was the pain of this latest revelation from Shenka. I have now dragged myself to my writing desk in order at least to record this hopefully final piece of information.

I feel pretty comprehensively betrayed but I am quick to comfort myself. 'I am in good company,' say I to myself. 'Margaret Thatcher, Julius Caesar and Jesus Christ himself were all profoundly betrayed by those closest to them.' O dear, there's my narcissism at work again!

The Revolving Door

Apart from the pivotal events in your life, the other big thing to reconsider in old age is your faith in God, or lack of it.

Old age is the last chance to change your mind about God. It is not too late. In fact it is the perfect opportunity because now you know a lot about life and you are in a position to judge. You have long since been aware that things very often are not what they appear to be. To arrive at the truth it can be necessary to turn apparent common sense on its head. Quantum physics, for example, does just that. Think of all of life's paradoxes. Giving is the best way of receiving, et cetera. The more you know about life, the more you realise how un-normal it is. It is, in fact, astounding. In my humble experience as that most materialistic entity, a common or garden businessman, I have learnt over my working career that it is the SPIRIT of a venture that will guarantee its success rather than its facts and figures. By success I mean fulfilment.

Kids Know Best

'You know nothing,' said Descartes, 'except that you exist.'

'I think, therefore I am,' was the only thing you could say for certain.

Obviously you don't know whether God exists and you certainly don't know whether He doesn't. Of course, Descartes would argue that you don't even know whether a table exists because all the evidence of its hard physical existence is merely sense data and your senses can be easily deceived.

The rest of us, who are not philosophers, say that it does not matter whether the table exists or not, what we do know is that it makes life a lot easier for us, even if it does not exist. I would argue the same about God. People and nations who experiment living without God find life a lot more difficult. Christendom, for all its faults, has given us a civilisation, which we have then exported all over the world. Our current secular lifestyle where self is put first, porn and drugs are normalised, abortion is justified, money is King and fame is God has resulted in the prescription of antidepressants going up five times in just thirty years.

I assume the reverse is true on the basis that two minuses make a plus. I know the real attitude of most contemporary Christians is that religion is all very well as long as it does not seriously affect your private life but supposing, hypothetically speaking, hedonism really was replaced by spirituality in the UK, presumably antidepressants would be reduced by five times in thirty years. That would be the effect of God. Such a transformation would make His existence worthy of serious consideration.

I maintain that adolescent atheism is due to mental inertia, just plain laziness and it is at that age that disbelief takes hold. Children naturally love the idea of God. You only have to listen to a teenagers' pathetically slack reasoning to realise that they have not given the subject sustained serious thought. And why on earth should they? There are a lot more pressing things on their mind such as popularity, exams, drink, drugs, music, romance and sex. I think the problem is that atheism becomes a habit of thought and that people feel they simply don't have time to reconsider this very intellectually demanding issue until old age.

Not even God can make Two plus Two equal Five

Is God just a placebo? Is He like Prozac? Or does God really exist? Let us seriously consider this question now that we have entered old age and we have got the time to think about it, especially since death is the next thing on the agenda. Actually, let us start by not being serious. Humour is a good way of opening us up to other possibilities. It is a great limbering up exercise. I will give you the best religious joke I know, a funny dream and a humorous exchange I had with an ardent atheist.

First the joke: Ronaldo, the footballer, was so astonished by his own amazing ability on the football field that he proclaimed to the world: 'I am a gift from God.' Messi, the marginally better player, replied: 'That's not true. Have you ever seen me give away anything.'

Second, the exchange: I admitted to this fellow that I believed in God.

'I believe in God.'

'Intelligent man like you?'

'What it takes to get a compliment!'

'No, really, Kit. Nobody of discernment, rationale and a general working intelligence can possibly believe in this ridiculous mental construct.'

'Ah, but I do.'

'Why?'

'Because it's easier. As you say, you need to be clever not to believe in Him. Only fools believe in God which is what I would expect of Him because if there was a God and he wants you to believe in Him and He is all inclusive, He would have to make it possible for even fools to believe in Him. St Paul says in his letter to the Corinthians that God did not necessarily recommend himself to the worldly wise or the mighty or the noble 'But God hath chosen the foolish things of the world to confound the wise.' In this respect, I am a happy to be a foolish thing.'

Now, the dream: I was having a chat with Ted Hughes and God. Pretty elevated company, although I say so myself. Ted Hughes was a genius and God is no slouch but in my dream I could keep up with them both. So there we were – the three of us – on a country walk.

'God, Ted, Kit.' We made our introductions, all the permutations. 'I don't know whether you have ever met? Ted, God, Kit . . . God, Kit, Ted . . . Kit, God, Ted.' We got talking and Ted was being very complimentary about nature and congratulated God on its creation and God said He enjoyed Ted's poetry. I didn't want to spoil the party or anything, although I did feel a little left out of this mutual admiration society, but anyway, I made it incumbent upon myself to draw attention to the incidence of mass starvation, torture, war and disease in the Second and Third Worlds and the epidemic of general and acute psychological distress in the affluent West and do you know what He said? God. Do you know what He said?

'Sorry.'

I thought about the dream afterwards and I thought you say

'Sorry' when there's nothing you can do about a thing, mostly because it has happened in the past and you cannot 'unhappen' something, or else you say 'Sorry' when you are about to do something in the future injurious to the person to whom you are apologising but you have no choice – like a surgeon saying to a patient: 'I am sorry we are going to have to operate on you and it will involve a painful convalescence.'

God is omnipotent but He is also part of reality. God Himself cannot make two plus two equal five. Sorry, but free will exists. Without it, we could not be human. We would be robots. Sorry, but the Devil exercised free will and chose to betray God. Sorry, but reality now includes the Devil, a separate force to God and unfortunately, the Devil has made suffering a part of life.

The present Pope Francis has said that the Devil's cleverest trick has been to persuade people that He doesn't even exist. It is typical of our soft and sanitised world, how Modern Man has been Disney-fied. Even most contemporary Christians balk at the notion of the Devil. They put him down to medieval superstition. Why? It takes as much of a leap of imagination to contemplate the existence of God as it does the Devil or to believe in Heaven as it is to believe in Hell.

Obviously if God exists, so does the Devil. Just look at nature, the mirror of reality. There is always an opposite: winter and summer, day and night, dark and light, hot and cold, up and down, good and evil, pleasure and pain, et cetera. So we have to put up with pain and atheists are so considerate that rather than blame God, they refuse to believe in Him. But God has so made the world that pain has its counterpoint in pleasure and both are finite. Suffering is relieved by death and death has been conquered by Christ, just like life has been made possible by God. Who says Life is not worth the agonies of childbirth? Who says the Afterlife is not worth the agonies of the death bed?

Religion is Nuts

Of course, a lot is asked of you, to believe in God. Religion is the opposite of common sense. It is a kind of madness. Love your enemy. Somebody slaps you across the cheek, offer the other cheek. Eat my body. Drink my blood. The meek are cool. Ultimate failure breeds success. Famous last words: 'Why have you abandoned me?' We are expected to devote our lives to a guy whose last words show he has been deserted by his principal backer. That is not a vote of confidence. We are supposed to love somebody we have never seen. We are asked to behave, quite frankly, like a lunatic setting aside time every day addressing thin air. Let's face it, prayer just looks as if you are talking to yourself and that is what mad men do.

Of course, if God does not exist, prayer is delusional in which case clergy, people who devote their lives to it, should in the course of their lives increasingly exhibit signs of neurotic and irrational behaviour, but the reverse appears to be the case. They may start off as rather gauche and enthusiastic idealists – what the world calls naïve – but they often end up as wise and holy men to whom we turn in times of crisis and to whom we call upon for words of wisdom at the most solemn moments of our lives, commemorating birth, marriage and death at baptisms, weddings and funerals. Wisdom and goodness do not come from a lie and if God does not exist, prayer is a lie.

Yes, the tabloids write about those rare priests who are corrupted because their readers' love scandal but certainly, in my experience, the top ten people I have met in my life, probably six have been priests.

Having said that, I agree that it is astonishing how such a barmy idea as religion has caught on. Billions of people transgressing hundreds of different cultures across the globe, indeed the vast majority of people, believe in what, on the face of it, appears to be an exercise in wishful thinking: Daddy in the Sky with Diamonds.

Religion is such a blatant fairy tale, complete with flappy things called angels for goodness sake.

All physical evidence points to the contrary. The outrageous unfairness of life, its random suffering on a macro and micro level, the indifference and brutality of nature, diseases with their own particular recipes of torture and the jokingly high levels of pain that accompany the experiences of birth and death. Darwin has proven beyond doubt that we are just a bunch of clever monkeys and we are now persuaded that the world came about as a result of an explosion in space billions of years ago.

Why then do nearly all of us believe in God? Especially in this most heathen of countries, a nation of mocking, scoffing sceptics and cynics, if ever there was one. Just look at our hilarious comedy shows and our fantastic history of satire programmes from *Monty Python* to *Mock the Week*. Even here, two thirds of British people believe in God. Of course, in more idealistic countries like the USA, Poland and Ireland it is over ninety per cent of the population.

Why? How can we possibly believe in somebody whom nobody has ever seen, when all we can say with any degree of probability was that there was once a guy, 2000 years ago who, according to his friends, claimed to be God, or at least God's son which, if you believed him, meant that God did exist because how could you be the son of somebody who did not exist?

Adam Ate Newton's Apple

Well, as mentioned before, the Devil explains suffering and actually Darwin can be said to deal with the issue of evolution. We might have started off as monkeys but we have ended up as humans, just like the way a fetus starts as a blob and ends up a baby. Thus, the abortionist feels, for example, no qualms about eliminating a ten-week fetus but would not get rid of a ten-week baby. According to the abortionist, the fetus is not a human being, but the baby is. It has evolved into one.

I do not subscribe to that point of view. I believe we evolved from monkeys as a result of divine intervention. There came a moment. There came an event, like the moment of creation which initiated the Big Bang. I believe in events like the event of Christ's death which brought about the miracle of resurrection not just for him but us as well. Death is not a gradual process, nor is conception. There is nothing to say that a monkey did not become a man in a moment, as immortalised in Michelangelo's illustration on the ceiling of the Sistine Chapel, when you see God's finger pointing at the finger of man and charging us with divine electricity.

You know the most exciting time for believers was when Isaac Newton came along and realised that every single thing in nature – that is the workings of man, all the myriad species, the world itself and the universe that binds it all together – obeyed some law or other. All was in order. From a fruit fly to a volcano, from a toe nail to a planet, from a brain cell to a sound wave, everything had a design. Nothing was random.

Everything was intentional. At this point I think of oil. Isn't it amazing that for centuries Arabs were wandering around the desert on top of lakes of liquid black stuff rather like molasses and if they ever came across it, they would have gone: 'Now what is the point of that?' 'Wait, my son, that underground ocean will eventually enable the modern world. Everything has a purpose. Nothing is without meaning.'

It was as if everything had been created by a Supreme Intelligence because, of course, we know from our own lives that where there is an order there is always somebody governing it. Chaos happens in anarchic situations when it is a free for all, like children without parental control.

Newton was a revelation. To the people at the time it was as if he was a scientific confirmation of the existence of The Creator. Before him, people never knew you could study these laws of nature, under-stand them and then create seemingly miraculous events yourself like television and aeroplanes and washing machines. All that has happened since is that subsequent scientists have discovered more and more complicated laws like quantum physics whose patterns of activity are increasingly difficult to comprehend, and that the furthermost reaches of knowledge are shrouded in mystery.

In fact, science is bringing us full circle. Obviously the circumstances of life have their beginnings in mystery. There never was a first moment because there was always one before it, so how do you get to now? There never was a last inch of space because there was an inch after it so how do you get to here? Atheists are obsessed by reason but rational thinking will never be able fully to explain the facts of life which, as described above, lie beyond our mind's comprehension. Theology takes over where science ends.

Marriage is not Reasonable

We are slaves to reason but that is only a relatively recent development. The well-known theologian, Karen Armstrong, devotes her whole book, *The Case for God*, to distinguishing the difference between mythos and logos. Up until the Age of Enlightenment in the eighteenth century, mythos held sway as the dominant way of thinking. Mythos is all about awe and wonder. Superstition is the corruption of that spirit. Mysticism is its finest expression. Mythos is one approach to knowledge and it plays to what you might call the feminine and intuitive instinct. Logos is the masculine and rational approach. Dogmatism is a corruption of that attitude; scholarship, its highest expression. Fundamentalism is a fusion of the worst of both approaches to knowledge.

Reason! Was it reason alone that made you chose your wife? It was not merely a calculation. It was also an act of faith, hope and love. Sacrificing your independence for a woman you don't really know and never really will, immersing yourself in her being and allowing her to surround you with her identity for the rest of your life – that decision is as big as your decision to give up your independence to God, and allow Him to overwhelm your consciousness in prayer. Of course, making an act of faith in God is more than just a rational decision, which is why you can be intellectually persuaded by the high probability of His existence and yet still resist the call to prayer – which I reckon accounts for most of the sixty-six per cent of people in the UK who proclaim a faith in God.

There are signs that confound the rational mind and point to the omnipresence of the Lord. Miracles, supernatural events, metaphysical experiences happen a lot more frequently that you could possibly imagine. According to Oxford University academic and author of an eleven-year-old study on happiness, Michael Argyle: 'A third of the population have had intense metaphysical experiences, such as a vision of the Virgin Mary.'

Thirty years ago, six children first clapped eyes on Our Lady just after 6 o'clock in the small village of Medjugorje in Croatia and four of them have been seeing her every day at that time since that portentous evening. The remaining two have completed the spiritual journey Our Lady has set for them and stopped seeing her a few years ago.

How can these six children, or middle-aged men and women as they are now, be hallucinating when they share the same vision and hear the same words that Our Lady gives them in her monthly messages to the faithful? How do they all drop to their knees at precisely the same moment when Our Lady first appears to them? How do their eyes all go to the same spot where Our Lady is appearing to them? How do they all snap out of their vision at the same micro-second? How come they have not been uncovered as frauds in thirty years of visions when they have been subjected to every test and every enquiry imaginable from theologians, psychotherapists and neuroscientists? How can they have successfully duped the 20 million pilgrims who have gone to Medjugorje to witness these people have their visions? These people are not accomplished spies, actors and con artists. Originally they were just ordinary schoolchildren. Now, of course, they are probably living saints. On 24 October 1985, Our Lady told the visionaries: 'Dear children, from day to day I wish to clothe you in sanctity.'

I first became interested in Medjugorje when I heard Our Lady was impressing upon the visionaries the need for people to pray for peace. I told my wife at the time that that meant that there was probably going to be a war in Yugoslavia, but I felt that was highly unlikely because this was Europe not the Middle East. Of course, a few years later that is precisely what happened. Medjugorje was a village that sat on the intersection between the newly formed states of Croatia, Bosnia and Serbia.

For suspiciously supernatural events you need look no further than the last four Popes. Pope John Paul I, the one they called the Smiling Pope, knew he was the wrong choice and famously said, on being elected by his fellow cardinals: 'May God forgive you for what you have just done.' He was dead thirty-three days later. Pope John Paul II was shot from point blank range and saved by a religious medal of Our Lady of Fatima. The bullet ricocheted off the medal, deflecting its full impact. The switch over from Pope Benedict XVI to Pope Francis I was marked by a spectacularly accurate strike of lighting that dramatically managed to hit the very pinnacle of St Peter's in Rome. It was a direct hit from heaven.

Look to your own friends and family and you will probably be aware of inexplicable things that have happened to at least one person in your immediate circle. A friend of our family's Veronica Weld Blundell's forty-two year-old daughter, Diana, had a fetus that was diagnosed with Edward's Syndrome which the doctors said would kill it at the latest within twenty-four hours of birth so there seemed no point in continuing the pregnancy, let alone going through the pain and trauma of childbirth for such little return, but nevertheless the mother refused an abortion. She was a Catholic.

A friend of the Weld Blundells, Jane Tempest, said she knew an Indian priest who had given Mother Teresa the last rites. He had kept her habit and chopped it up into lots of little crosses which he sealed in plastic cards. The Weld Blundells got one of these relics and used to put it on Diana's womb and prayed over it every day that remained of the pregnancy. The doctors said that the baby might at any moment die in the womb. Every time they put the relic on the womb, the baby would indicate he was still alive by kicking. Amazingly, the baby was born with nothing wrong with it. He is still alive today. Sounds nutty, doesn't matter. It's true.

I find it hilarious but strangely touching to see footballers make a sign of the cross as they come on to the pitch in international football matches. They honestly think God is going to give them a good game, as if God hasn't got more pressing things to do than interfere in a European cup-tie. See God up there receiving all those millions of prayers – you know, a lot of desperate pleas: 'God, save me from despair!' and millions of people in the Third World saying: 'O God I'm starving!' and people like the Pope praying like a hippy for peace and love. And then suddenly: 'What's that? What's that?' It's a footballer taking a penalty kick:

> 'Bless this ball that I boot
> Into the net by any route.
> Come on, God, don't let me down,
> I'm right out here on my own.'

The amount of doggerel God has to put up with. People seem to imagine their prayer has got a better chance of success if it rimes. It is pure superstition, no other word for it – otherwise Rangers would never have won the Scottish League nine times in a row!

Actually, to tell you the truth, I have had my sporting moment where God must have interrupted a busy schedule to give me a helping hand because there is no way I could possibly have done it on my own. And I can't even say it was a crunch match. Yes, the

Sky Sports of the day never broadcast the historic cricket match between Moreton Hall and Nowton Court Prep Schools under-elevens, the summer of 1964.

I was very religious when I was ten. It was just a phase I was going through and it lasted a summer term at school. I would spend all my breaks in the chapel and pray for success at cricket. The typed team sheet for the first school match of the season was pinned up on the green felt board and I was surprised to find that I had not even been selected but the next day one of our team went down with an ankle injury and I was chosen to replace him.

We had gone into bat first and scored about 80 runs. When they started to bat, they were knocking our four bowlers all over the park and then our team captain asked if anybody else could bowl and I put my hand up. Before each bowl I did a public sign of the cross and a speedy Hail Mary and then got a wicket. I got five people out in five balls, which I discovered, half a dozen years later, was a world record. I looked it up in the *Guinness Book of Records*. Unbelievably, I wasn't mentioned but some other geezer who only took four wickets in as many balls.

Could you Sleep after the Exorcist?

It is extraordinary how atheists are quite happy to accept that evil exists and yet fail to follow through as to what exactly that means. We watch horror movies. We have nightmares and we are scared of murderers. I have a friend, Frances Butler-Schloss, who as a lawyer briefly came into contact with Peter Sutcliffe, the Yorkshire Ripper, on a prison visit and she said the hairs stood up at the back of her neck.

There was a prison inmate called John Anderson serving seven years for attempted murder although he was acquitted of raping five females, two of them children due to lack of proof. I was struck by this newspaper comment: 'Anderson was terrified that someone was trying to kill him. And the officers tasked with keeping him alive and getting him to court were changed regularly – not because of security, but because they couldn't stand being near him for more than five minutes.'

Yes, we all know evil exists and I will tell you a little secret. It is spiritual. People say about particularly bad behaviour. 'O he behaved like an animal!' Animals do not go in for gratuitous massacre or cunning manipulation or sadistic bullying or vindictive retaliation or all the other horrible things people can do to another in extremis in moments of sheer badness. No, animals are not evil, they are just thoughtless. You have got to be a spiritual to be evil.

The opposite exists as well and it is called holiness. 'Those of us who have met them, know that there is in a saint's life an extraordinary and almost palpable power of good which is unlike 'virtue',' wrote A. N. Wilson.

You must see the three part TV series *The Monastery* about five urbane, attractive, successful men spending forty days as novitiate monks at Worth's Benedictine Monastery. Their thin veneer of sophistication disintegrated in days. The film showed how the men from the world were like children compared to the monks. The effect of the world for all their success in it seemed to have retarded their development as people. Not only did they have problems getting on with one another, but also they had none of the monks' charisma. – acquired, not inherited, because you could see that genetically they had a lot more going for them than the monks.

They got a lot more real as the days wore on and they came to grips with their inner demons. Furious or bored with one another, they were always disarmed by the monks who immediately made them smile, or laugh outright or contemplate their difficulties with perspective. In a classic fight or flight confrontation with a fellow visitor, one guy fled the room in a rage and ran to his bedroom. He was immediately followed by a monk who had him laughing at himself, literally within minutes.

If spirituality exists, the embodiment of which we see in holy and evil people, then that must mean the invisible world of the spirit exists. There is a dimension to existence that exceeds the animal kingdom. Another way of saying the same thing is that you can feel spiritual just as you can feel social. They are two different moods. I would argue that feeling social indicates that other people exist just as feeling spiritual indicates that God exists.

I'm always highly principled in the mornings but it can be a very different matter late at night with a drink having been taken, a lovely woman opposite and a bunch of fellow ribald revellers egging one another on to better one another in the highly competitive field of social exchange. At times like these, morality seems pretty staid stuff. I think possibly I lack consistency. Two different moods, same person: spiritual in the morning, social late at night with, dare I say it, a little touch of the sexual.

We know from experience that we have been so designed that every feeling has a reason. If we did not feel hungry, we would not eat and therefore die. I remember feeling sexy when I was about eight and not knowing what it meant. Nobody had told me about intercourse and so I had no idea that without it the human race would come to an end. I just had a dream one night about girls in grass skirts and I was concerned enough to tell my mother about it in the morning. I said I had felt during the dream ready to burst. I was disappointed that she, extraordinarily enough, seemed to be suppressing a smile. All I knew was that here was a new quite alarming feeling that was important. I was right. Similarly, you feel spiritual. It is important. It has a big meaning.

Mind the Gap

Hollowness is also an important feeling, full of meaning. It is telling you that there is something big missing in your life. 'I had stopped mainlining chocolate,' wrote journalist Jinni Roddy in a *Sunday Times* article about the benefits of neural therapy. 'The feeling of wanting to plug up the hole in my soul lessens.' People are in a desperate search to plug that hole and they will go to any extreme. Jinni has even gone to the lengths of giving up chocolate!

Dr George Carey, Anglican Archbishop of Canterbury points to more conventional methods. 'Western culture is obsessed with three alternative saviours – therapy, education and wealth – none of which can provide lasting healing for our broken world.' The only thing that gave solace to my friends, neighbours and confirmed atheists, Roddy and Katrina Beaton in the immediate aftermath of their terrible tragedy when they lost their son and two grandchildren in an horrendous canoeing accident on the West Coast was to go for walks in nature – as holy a place as a church.

Film stars, above all, have got to be perfect in mind and body. They have to achieve the serenity of a saint and the poise of porcelain, at least in public, while they are going through endless chat shows and press interviews to promote their latest films. They have their images to project. Physical exercise gives you calm as well as fitness. 'I had to put a lot of work in at the gym, which I loathe going to. It is all too easy for the film industry to conclude that an actress is past their best,' said Catherine Zeta Jones at her high court libel case against *Hello* magazine.

What friend and fellow gallivanter, Julie Cameron said about the rich in London is to a lesser extent true of everybody. 'They are all on something,' she said. Most people try and fill the hole with a combination of or a selection from drink, drugs, money, work, television, internet, play station, sex, antidepressants or some wacky cult but the problem is with this strategy is that it is like pouring water into a hole in the sand. It fills up alright but seeps away pretty quickly. Only prayer works, boring though you may think it is.

Of course, I hear you say: 'Friends! It is friends that give life meaning.' Forget this romantic tosh. Let's get real. You know perfectly well their affection is conditional. You are thankful for these fond alliances but essentially you are on your own, bar God.

Somerset Maugham wrote in *The Moon and Sixpence* about a man who had abandoned mainstream civilisation to live on a deserted island and explained how he had coped without a social life:

> *Évidemment*, it is not exciting on my island, and we are very far from the world – imagine, it takes four days to come to Tahiti – but we are happy here. It is given to few men to attempt a work and to achieve it. Our life is simple and innocent. We are untouched by ambition, and what pride we have is due only to our contemplation of the work of our hands. Malice cannot touch us, nor envy attack. Ah *mon cher monsieur*, they talk of the blessedness of labour, and it is a meaningless phrase, but to me it has the most intense significance. I am a happy man.

'I am sure, you deserve to be,' I smiled.

'I wish I could think so. I do not know how I have deserved to have a wife who was the perfect friend and helpmate, the perfect mistress and the perfect mother.'

I reflected for a while on the life that the Captain suggested to my imagination. 'It is obvious that to lead such an existence and make so great a success of it, you must both have needed a strong will and determined character.'

'Perhaps; but without one other factor we could have achieved nothing.'

'And what was that?'

He stopped , somewhat dramatically, and stretched out his arm.

'Belief in God. Without that we should have been lost.'

Robinson Crusoe was of the same opinion.

No Amount of Monkeys can Write Shakespeare

Because I am a business man I don't get carried away by promise of rich reward unsupported by hard evidence, I am about as mystic as a clod of earth. My approach to God is overwhelmingly calculated. The art of business is realising the difference between big and little.

I know that God is big and so I have spent a lot of time thinking, reading and writing about the issue and I am further persuaded by two other pragmatic observations.

'Scientists say that if the values of the natural constants – for example the average distance between stars – had varied only slightly in either direction, our universe could not have been hospitable to life. Our presence here is dependent on hundreds of numerical accidents. Had any one of them varied a fraction, no conscious human being could have existed to gaze back over the long odyssey we have travelled from the first great burst of energy,' wrote John Cornwell in a *Sunday Times* review of a book called *Stardust* by John Gribbin.

What John Cornwell is saying is that the planet Earth is, to all intents and purposes, a statistical impossibility for the circumstances of its creation to have happened by accident. It is about infinity to one against. Now, as I have indicated before, I am a betting man – all businessmen are because where there's money there's risk. I am not going to bet on impossible odds, except the alternative is just as bad. The alternative to accidental creation is, of course, the hand of God. It is fluke against magic.

But even if fluke had miraculously produced Earth, how could it then produce the marvel of man? 'You would not expect a random collection of chemicals suddenly to organise themselves into a human being,' wrote John Cornwell in the same article. And, what is more, what we know about fluke is that it has no meaning and yet life is full of meaning. What is the meaning of life? It is the greatest question we ask ourselves for that very reason. We innately know life has meaning.

If Earth was a fluke, why is it so heartbreakingly beautiful in every particle of its myriad variety of creation? If I had to imagine divine creative genius, I could not come up with a more amazing product than this phenomenal interplay of animal, vegetable and mineral. A car crash is an accident and it doesn't look very pretty.

I do not subscribe to the view that if you give an infinity of monkeys an infinity of time and a typewriter, one of them would eventually write Shakespeare. I prefer to believe in Shakespeare.

Is Christ a Liar?

I don't think Christ was a liar. Mandela never said he was the Son of God. You only have to read the New Testament, corroborated by four different journalists – Mathew, Mark, Luke and John, if you will – to realise that from what Christ reputedly said and did, he was an extraordinary man blessed with the finest expression of that magnificent trinity of the mind: brain, heart and soul.. The nearest equivalent we have produced in our time has been Nelson Mandela. Can you imagine if Mandela had come out of prison and said to the world's press, 'I am God.' We would have thought he had gone nuts in jug.

There is nothing to indicate in his behaviour during the three years of his ministry that Christ had gone mad; in fact – the very reverse. His teachings were so full of wisdom that they have formed the basis of civilisation, of which we have been the beneficial recipients from that day to this. And his actions were nothing short of heroic. No, he was super sane.

If a man of that calibre and that integrity says he is the Son of God, you just better believe him.

Is Life just Monkey Business?

If God does not exist, you are just a monkey; a clever one admittedly, but still a monkey. Why then do we have a conscience? How come there exists in our interior worlds a thing called morality? Dostoyevsky was right when he wrote that without God you can do what you want and yet we all – believers and non-believers – feel a sense of right and wrong. The Amises would dismiss that feeling merely as social conditioning. Morality is sentimentality. They are desperately trying to show a way of life divorced from morality and recommend it on the grounds that it is the only true, honest and accurate way for an atheist to live. They are absolutely right.

Celebrity Endorsements

We live in the Age of Celebrity and it would be remiss of me not to give you some celebrity quotes on the subject. I have chosen some unlikely people: Keynes, the father of modern economics; the comedian Russell Brand, the most salacious man on the planet; D. H. Lawrence, and, finally, another well-known author, Alice Thomas Ellis, simply for the quality of her quote.

J. M. Keynes wrote of his post-First World War contemporaries: 'I begin to see that our generation owed a great deal to our fathers' religion. And the young who are brought up without it will never get so much out of life. They're trivial: like dogs after their own lusts.'

Modern day, Russell Brand said: 'Because I don't think it possible to recover from drugs and alcohol without a spiritual aspect to life, an acceptance that any individual is powerless, that there is a God, a benign and loving God, that doesn't have to be doctrinaire, although it could be.'

The globally successful Alcoholics Anonymous twelve-step programme is based on that very observation. Alcoholics cannot afford the luxury of not believing in God. They need all the help they can get to beat their addiction. They need a power stronger than drink and AA has found that to be God, or a 'Higher Power' as they call Him.

D. H. Lawrence wrote the following exchange in *Women in Love*, written in the middle of the First World War in which he says life is pointless without God: 'Where in does life centre for you?'

'I don't know – that's what I want somebody to tell me. As far as I can make out, it doesn't centre at all. It is artificially held together by the social mechanism.'

'I know,' he said. 'It just doesn't centre. The old ideals are dead as nails – nothing there.'

'And you mean if there isn't the women, there's nothing.'

'Pretty well that – seeing there's no God.'

Sixties writer, Alice Thomas Ellis's conversion came about as a result of her thinking that she 'no longer found it possible to disbelieve in God.'

Dawkins in the Dock

My Uncle Pie once had to give Maggie Thatcher a briefing about alternative energy and he was advised to be very concise. Thatcher could not bear waffle. In fact, she claimed that there was no idea in the world so complicated you could not summarise it on one side of an A4 piece of paper. It is a habit I have got into when putting together a business plan for potential investors.

I set myself the same constraint after I read Richard Dawkins' *The God Delusion*, the book that attempted to debunk the whole idea of God. Dawkins' book has been an incredible success and is now known as 'the atheist's handbook'. Here follows my reply on one side of an A4 and you can judge for yourself whether I have dealt with Dawkins' scepticism. In his defence, he is not a theologian so he must be given some latitude, but then neither am I. We both use the same weapon: common sense. It is like we have dispensed with guns and swords. It's a bare knuckle punch-up. So here goes.

Life is mystery because there never was a first moment and there is no end to space. We live in infinity. Both Darwin and Einstein subscribed to a sense of awe and wonder about the mystery of life – that which is beyond our comprehension: what the mystics call the Cloud of Unknowing.

Dawkins disagrees. He thinks, given time, science will explain everything.

Well, according to scientists, the chance of planet Earth – this Garden of Eden capable of supporting life in its myriad forms –

actually existing is about infinity to one against. Dawkins calls it a fluke. But then you put man in the middle capable of appreciating it all. It's so wonderful, it makes you think it was intended.

Dawkins says religion is responsible for murder and mayhem down the ages. You could say the same about education. Without education, Hitler and Stalin would not have gained mastery over their peoples. Religion, like education, is just a source of power that can be abused, as it invariably is by fundamentalists.

Incidentally, Dawkins does not have a problem with suffering within the context of religious belief – and he is right. If you believe in God, writes Dawkins, it is logically sound to attribute suffering to 'a separate evil god, call him Satan'.

You cannot know God any more than a dog can know man. God is supernatural. Man is human. Dog is animal. These are three different levels of existence. Dawkins, of course, thinks you are just a monkey.

But just because we were once monkeys, it does not mean we still are.

How does a monkey become a human being? Either in a moment or gradually. The case for it all having happened in a moment is that the crucifixion of Christ happened in a moment and that, according to Christian teaching, enabled resurrection and made us superhuman, i.e., immortal. Another earlier moment of divine intervention in our development could have turned us from animal to human.

The gradualist argument is that evolution mirrors in very slow motion what abortionists imagine happens to the fetus as it gradually goes from blob to baby.

Dawkins' entire atheistic philosophy is based on evolution and the theory of the Selfish Gene. So morality is meaningless. Conscience is merely a product of inhibition. Altruism he dismisses as just 'an evolutionary misfiring'. Cop out.

Obviously, Dawkins says you do not have a soul. What you may think is spirituality is just aesthetics. But holiness exists, as does evil. These are spiritual qualities. They prove the existence of the spirit just like comedy proves the existence of humour or sexiness proves the existence of sex.

And obviously the practice of spirituality: prayer is totally delusional if God does not exist but why do we turn to the clergy for words of wisdom in times of need when their very profession is based on a lie? Wisdom only comes from the truth. Why are registry office weddings and humanist funerals such functional affairs? What's missing?

Do you really think you are a monkey? Why do we have an innate sense of right and wrong? Intuitively, you know you are not an animal. You are totally different, You are a human being: 'a little lower than an angel'. The proof of the pudding is Venice. God didn't make that and I bet He's envious.

Conclusion

'The fundamental striving of every man should be to create for himself an inner freedom towards life and to prepare for himself a happy old age,' wrote the famous Eastern guru, Gurdjieff.

Somebody who, according to Gurdjieff's estimation, could be considered a notable success was our elderly next door neighbour, a priest, Canon Stone – born in our local village, Beauly. He was, for a long time, its priest, but latterly he moved five miles up the road to Dingwall- a man, in short, not widely travelled. He was an obvious saint. You could tell almost immediately on meeting him. He had a simplicity about him that cut to the chase. He summed me up in one phrase, and he had only briefly met me. 'Ah, Kit, you try too hard.' And he didn't mean it as a compliment. It was like I was a car in the wrong gear.

He seemed to live on the brink of laughter while at the same time conscious of the onerous cares of the world. After all, he was a long-serving priest on the receiving end of thousands of confessions.

I remember the day Canon Stone had been called in to give my father the sacrament of Extreme Unction just before he was due to go under the knife in an operation that would probably kill him. We had no choice because the alternative was certain death. So, as you can imagine, it was an emotionally charged event for the family grouped around my father's hospital bed.

My father indicated he wanted to say something to my mother. She leant over to hear the last words of the great man and she fled the room in tears. It transpired, we later discovered, that he had said: 'Don't forget the rhones.' (That's the Scottish word for gutters). It was Autumn and he was concerned they would get clogged up with leaves and create a problem with damp for the house if they were not cleared. Into this scene of high drama stepped Canon Stone.

His attitude was refreshing. His whole demeanour seemed to express the idea that death was not a tragedy. It was not extinction. It was just a rite of passage like birth, baptism, confirmation and marriage, for which solemn events the Church provided corresponding Holy Sacraments.

There were the waiting surgeons, the fleeing wife, the anxious family and the priest going about his business. It was a moment when time stood still: the inevitable had to wait.

That was the serious face of Canon Stone but otherwise he was mostly at play. I remember one time we got him over for lunch with a friend and neighbour of mine, Joe Gibbs, a highly intelligent agnostic, almost atheist, who wanted to grill him about some of the apparent inconsistencies in religion but within minutes of sitting down at the table, Joe was disarmed. Joe's opener for ten was: 'And the Holy Trinity: three Gods in one. What's that all about?'

'I haven't got a clue,' said Canon Stone, sixty years a priest, grinning from ear to ear. 'It's a total mystery to me!' The lunch shortly degenerated into a merry meal with religion a quickly abandoned subject.

Canon Stone died a year ago and the person who reminds me of him most is my nine month old grandson, Finn – the fellow who was born at the start of this book. Nobody does joy quite like Finn.

I remember at his christening the other week at Corpus Christi Church in Brixton with four other babies: two Winston Churchills, a wriggler and a wailer, and their respective families. Then there was our handsome little prince doing the baby equivalent of drumming his fingers and looking at his wrist watch, wondering when the action was due to start.

There he sat in his mother's arms in one of the front pews, turning round for a word here and a word there, which is all he could do because his vocabulary does not stretch beyond 'la' and 'gnu'.

Then there came his grand moment. The other four babies got dunked in the font and when recovered from the reverse position immediately buried their heads into their mothers' arms. Finn, on the other hand, performed a classic Madonna and Child pose, his face facing outwards for the thirty or so mobile phone cameras pointed at him by ancestry on both sides of his family from the wall opposite. He sat bolt upright, actually in his father's arms, his face beaming with joy and he held that toothless smile for a solid minute and the whole church laughed.

Finn's face is full of joy and so was Canon Stone's. One is born of innocence. The other was finally earned in old age after a tough life well spent.